Living in the USA

3 A competency-based novel for advanced intermediate students of English

Judy Burghart

National Textbook Company
a division of NTC/CONTEMPORARY PUBLISHING GROUP
Lincolnwood, Illinois USA

To Catalina Paige

Project Editor:	Kathleen Schultz
Designer:	Linda Snow Shum
Cover and interior illustrations:	Sandra Burton

ISBN: 0-8442-7696-0

Published by National Textbook Company,
a division of NTC/Contemporary Publishing Group, Inc.,
4255 West Touhy Avenue,
Lincolnwood (Chicago), Illinois 60712-1975 U.S.A.

11 12 13 14 VRS/VRS 0 5 4 3 2

Contents

Introduction

Living in the U.S.A. is a three-book series of competency-based novels for young adult and adult students of English at the beginning intermediate, intermediate, and advanced intermediate levels. These novels are designed to meet students' specific needs in two separate, but equally important, areas—survival skills and language skills. The series reinforces and enhances the competencies that are taught in the adult English language classroom while presenting students with the type of developmental and consequential events that characterize a novel.

Students are introduced to the main characters, Ted and Janet Parker, and are invited to share their experiences in a series of everyday situations. Each chapter focuses on a specific event and includes a practical "how-to" solution for a common problem or issue the Parkers confront and resolve.

The general competencies explored include such issues as housing, health, employment, consumer education, money skills, clothing, transportation, community resources, home safety, legal rights, and government and law. Through Ted and Janet Parker, students will learn about specific life skills such as understanding store coupons, entering an emergency clinic, understanding a time card, using the newspaper, understanding fire hazards in the home, reading a bus schedule, using the state unemployment office, opening a checking account, and reporting a burglary.

The **Living in the U.S.A.** series is also a carefully graded course of grammar, vocabulary, and idioms. The exercises at the end of each chapter emphasize all four language skills and offer students an enjoyable way to relate the important places and events they are reading about to their own daily lives.

Life Skills Chart

Chapter	Specific Competencies
Chapter 1 **Cross Out Line Number 10**	• Using classified ads • Altering rental agreements • Understanding renter/landlord responsibilities
Chapter 2 **How about Your Cheapest?**	• Understanding monthly payments, interest, penalties
Chapter 3 **On the Floor?**	• Ordering at a restaurant • Tipping
Chapter 4 **With You Alone**	• Making flight reservations • Understanding reconfirming
Chapter 5 **It Must Be Inflation**	• Understanding income vs. bills and needs and wants • Making a budget
Chapter 6 **It's Not Enough**	• Understanding information on a pay stub
Chapter 7 **A Good Catch**	• Looking for a better job • Using the state employment office • Interviewing

General Competency	Grammar
Housing	• Articles • Comparative and superlative degrees of adjectives
Consumer Education	• Articles • Comparison of adverbs • Question word order
Consumer Education	• Infinitives • **To be able to** • Adjectives and adverbs
Consumer Education	• Indirect objects • Objects of prepositions • Adjective clauses
Money Skills	• Tag questions • **Used to**
Employment	• Negative questions • **Have to**
Employment	• Gerunds • Past vs. past continuous

Life Skills Chart

Chapter	Specific Competencies
Chapter 8 **What This Independent Woman Needs**	• Opening a checking account • Understanding minimal balance • Understanding a signature card
Chapter 9 **Twenty Dollars Is Just Right**	• Repairing a conventional faucet • Explaining a **how-to** job
Chapter 10 **Make It Light**	• Understanding food labels • Understanding nutrition
Chapter 11 **About Four Loads**	• Understanding clothing labels and washing instructions
Chapter 12 **Don't Touch Anything**	• Reporting a burglary • Burglar-proofing a home
Chapter 13 **I Could Have Screamed**	• Filing a claim • Functioning of small-claims courts
Chapter 14 **A Little Worse**	• Dealing with a police officer • Learning about traffic school
Chapter 15 **I'd Marry You**	

General Competency	Grammar
Money Skills	• Expressions of purpose • **Would rather/had better**
Housing	• **Say/tell** • Present perfect • Present perfect continuous • **Be/do**
Health	• Present perfect vs. past • **For/since**
Consumer Education	• **Either/neither** • Conditional future possible
Housing	• **So/too** • Conditional present unreal
Legal Rights	• **Supposed to** • **Could have** + past participle
Legal Rights	• Passive voice • Grammar/vocabulary/idiom review

Meet the Parkers

This is Ted Parker, and this is Janet Parker. They're a young married couple who live in San Diego, California.

Ted works for Sun Valley Fruit Company. He's an assistant manager and generally works in the office. Janet recently started a new job. She used to work in computer sales. Now she works part-time as an instructor's aide in computer classes at a local high school.

Ted loves sports. He likes to golf, jog, and play baseball. Janet loves romantic movies. She likes to go for long walks along the beach. Janet also enjoys going jogging with Ted.

The Parkers are living in an apartment, but they're not very happy there. It's too noisy. Ted and Janet would like to find a quiet rental house. Would you like to know what they're planning to do? Let's go over to their apartment and find out.

CHAPTER 1

Cross Out Line Number 10

Vocabulary

agreement (n)   contract

available (adj)   ready

hunt (v)   look for

impolite (adj)   rude, not polite

included (adj)   a part of

initial (v)   write the first letters of one's first and last names

landlady (n)   owner (female)

landlord (n)   owner (male)

tenant (n)   renter

unfurnished (adj)   having no furniture

walk-through (n)   an inspection of an apartment or house

Idioms

Let's **look over** the agreement.   check

I'll **cross out** line number 10.   cancel

We would like to **think** it **over**.   think about, consider

Of course.   Sure.

Hold your horses, Janet.   wait, be patient

3

Cross Out Line Number 10

Ted and Janet decided to look for a new place to live. Their apartment complex was becoming noisier and noisier. Neighbors were giving wild parties. Stereos were getting louder.

The noise wasn't the only problem. The laundry room and the pool were getting dirtier, too. The grass wasn't cut, and there was trash in the parking lot. The whole apartment complex was getting messier.

"And the manager is very rude," Ted said. "The old manager was more polite than this new one. I think it's time for us to move, Janet."

"Me, too. Let's look for a little house on a quiet street in this neighborhood. Then we won't be bothered by rude neighbors."

They opened the newspaper to the classified section and looked under Unfurnished Houses. There was a long list of available houses in the area, but Janet circled only a few.

"Let's begin looking at the most inexpensive places. Okay, honey?" she asked. With her pencil, Janet circled three promising ads:

Great location 2BR/1BA, Lg eat in kit. New garage. D/W Sec dep req. 1 yr lease, $725/mo. Avail now. Call 555-4621	Sm 2BR, $700/mo. Cpt, drps, refrig, stv. Sundeck. Near trans, shops. No pets. 555-0098 Ben	**MOVE RIGHT IN Only $750/mo. Older 2BR/ 1½BA. Water/trash incl. Fenced yd. 555-4360

Ted got on the phone and made appointments with the landlords and landladies. The Parkers went hunting for a house that very afternoon.

The Parkers are now at one of the rental houses. They're talking to the landlady.

LANDLADY: Hello. I'm Jeannie Beck, the owner. Well, this is it. It's a wonderful little house for a young couple. Let's go in.

4

JANET: Oh, my! The house is much bigger than it looks from the outside.

TED: Not bad. Ms. Beck, will you steam clean the carpets?

LANDLADY: Of course. I'm going to paint, too. My last tenants were the worst! Very dirty people.

JANET: Did you say the utilities were included in the rent, Ms. Beck?

LANDLADY: Please call me Jeannie. Only the water and trash, not the gas and electric.

TED: What deposits are required, Jeannie?

LANDLADY: A security deposit of three hundred dollars and a cleaning deposit of fifty dollars. I also require the first and last months' rent.

JANET: There's a broken window in the master bedroom. What about the window, Jeannie?

LANDLADY: I'll take care of it. If you decide to take the place, we'll have a walk-through before you move in. I'll write down all the needed repairs. One of you and I will sign the list, and I'll fix everything before you move in. How's that?

JANET: Terrific. When is the rent due?

LANDLADY: On the first of every month.

TED: Do we need to sign a lease?

LANDLADY: No, but you'll have to sign a month-to-month agreement. I'll also need a written thirty-day notice before you move out. I have a copy of the contract with me. Would you like to check it?

JANET: I like this house, Ted. It's old, but it's roomier and more comfortable than our apartment. Let's look over the agreement.

Ted takes the rental agreement from the landlady.

TED: It says here that we can't put any nails in the walls. It's number 10 in the contract, Jeannie. Can you change that? We'd like to hang some pictures.

LANDLADY: Sure. No problem. I'll just cross out line number 10 and write my initials by it. You'll have to initial it, too.

JANET: Let's take the house, Ted. I love it.

TED: Hold your horses, Janet. Not so fast. We have other houses to see. Jeannie, will you take a check for one hundred dollars to hold the house for us? My wife and I would to think it over and tell you for sure tomorrow.

LANDLADY: That's fine with me. I hope you'll decide to take it.

JANET: Oh, we will. We will! This is the most exciting thing to happen to us today. Bye, Jeannie. Talk to you tomorrow.

Exercises

A. Answer the questions in complete sentences.

1. Why did the Parkers want to move?

2. What kind of house did they want?

3. Where did they look for ads?

4. What will Jeannie Beck do to the carpets?

5. What utilities were included?

6. When is the rent due?

7. What kind of agreement do Ted and Janet need to sign?

8. Is it possible to change a rental agreement? How?

B. True or false   Read each sentence. Write **T** on the line if the sentence is true. Write **F** on the line if it is false.

_____ 1. A landlord or landlady is an owner of a rental house.

_____ 2. A walk-through is a month-to-month agreement.

_____ 3. Your initials spell your last name.

_____ 4. To hunt for something is to look for it.

_____ 5. If an apartment is available now, it is ready for you to move in.

_____ 6. If you cross out number 10, you cancel it.

_____ 7. Utilities are pieces of furniture.

_____ 8. A rude person is polite.

_____ 9. A tenant pays rent.

_____ 10. An unfurnished house has no furniture in it for the renter.

C. **Articles** Complete each sentence with **a, an,** or **the.**

1. They're hunting for _____ quiet house.

2. _____ house they rented has two bedrooms.

3. _____ old manager was nicer.

4. She looked in _____ classified ads for _____ apartment.

5. Are _____ utilities included?

6. _____ rent is due on _____ first of each month.

7. There's _____ broken window in the living room.

8. Do we need to sign _____ agreement or _____ lease?

9. Let's take _____ house. I love it.

10. Do you like to live in _____ house or _____ apartment?

D. Comparative/superlative degrees of adjectives
Complete each sentence with the correct form of the adjective. Use **the** or **than** where necessary. Follow the examples:

Their stereo is ___louder than___ ours. (loud)
Their stereo is ___the loudest___ one in the complex.
(loud)

1. The laundry room is getting _____ and
   _____ . (dirty)

2. It's much _____ it looks from the outside. (large)

3. These apartments are _____ in the whole city.
   (cheap)

4. A two-bedroom apartment is _____ a one-bedroom.
   (expensive)

5. They want to live on _____ street in the city. (quiet)

6. The old manager was _____ the new one. (polite)

7. The house is much _____ their apartment.
   (comfortable)

8. Those tenants are getting _____ and
   _____ . (rude)

9. It's _____ to find a furnished house _____ it
   is to find an unfurnished one. (difficult)

10. Their house is _____ place in the neighborhood.
    (roomy)

E. Look at the ads below, then read the questions. Write the letter of the correct answer on the line.

a. Studio, walk-in closet, unfurn, cpt, drps. Util incl. No pets. $450/mo. Call 555-8990 or 555-8875

b. Lg 1 bdrm, D/W, A/C, Avail now. $500/mo. $250 sec dep req. 778 Gary St. See mgr.

c. Sm. sunny house, furn. 1BR, 1½BA. No pets. Older person pref. 555-0243

d. Modern house Avail Apr 1. 2BR, 2BA, stv, refrig. Lg yd for pet. 555-3367

_____ 1. Which rental has no bedroom?

_____ 2. Which rental is not ready until April?

_____ 3. Which rental requires a security deposit?

_____ 4. Which rental would like to have a senior citizen move in?

_____ 5. Which rentals do not allow pets?

_____ 6. Which rental has air conditioning?

_____ 7. Which rental has furniture?

_____ 8. If you have a dog, which rental will you look at?

F. Ask your partner   Practice asking and answering questions with a partner. You are interested in renting an apartment. Read these instructions and ask the correct questions. Your partner must answer in complete sentences. Then, have your partner ask you the questions.

1. Ask when the rent is due.

2. Ask how much the security deposit is.

3. Ask if the utilities are included.

4. Ask if the landlord will cross out line number 10.

5. Ask if Ms. Beck will take a check for one hundred dollars to hold the apartment.

6. Ask if you need to give a thirty-day notice before you move.

7. Ask if you need to sign a month-to-month agreement.

8. Ask if you may have a walk-through on Monday.

9. Ask where the laundry room is.

10. Ask if the apartment complex has a pool.

G.   Conversation   How about you?

1. Do you rent or own?

2. How many bedrooms does your home have?

3. Do you prefer to live in the city or in the suburbs? Why?

4. Explain how homes in your country are different from homes here.

5. Did you have any pets in your country? How about here?

CHAPTER 2

How about Your Cheapest?

Vocabulary

approve (v)   authorize, pass, say something is okay

argue (v)   fight verbally (with words)

broken-down (adj)   not useful, not functioning

bumpy (adj)   having bumps or lumps

couch (n)   sofa

insist (v)   maintain and repeat an opinion

penalty (n)   an extra charge for missing a payment

reasonable (adj)   inexpensive

sagging (adj)   sinking, making a depression

worn-out (adj)   old from use

Idioms

We just **broke** it **in**.   made comfortable from use

Ted would not **give in to** Janet.   let a person have what he or she wants

You did that **on purpose**.   intentionally

We're **settled in**.   comfortably set in a new place

What if we want to **pay** it **off** early?   pay the total remaining cost of an item

13

How about Your Cheapest?

"I love this little old house, Ted," Janet said. "I'm so glad we moved out of that terrible apartment complex. Now that we're settled in, all we need is a new sofa."

"What? What do you mean—new sofa?" Ted questioned. "What's wrong with the one we have?"

Janet explained to Ted that she thought their couch was ugly and worn-out. "We need a new one," she said.

"How can you say that, Janet? It's not broken-down. We just broke it in! It's comfortable. I can sit on this sofa more comfortably than on any other piece of furniture in the house."

Janet insisted that the sofa was no good. She told Ted that it was bumpy. She showed him a big, sagging depression where he always sat.

"I know," Ted answered. "I like to sit there. It fits me just right." Ted sat down in the sagging area. "I can sit here very comfortably and restfully. We don't need a new one," he insisted.

Ted and Janet argued over the sofa a few minutes more, but Ted would not give in to Janet.

"Okay, Ted," she finally said. "You win. We'll keep this old sofa. Let's not argue anymore. I don't want to fight."

Janet went over to her husband to sit on his lap and give him a big kiss. Just as she sat on him, two legs of the sofa broke. The weight of the two of them together was too much for the old couch.

"Janet!" Ted shouted. "You did that on purpose! You wanted to break the legs!"

Ted gently pushed his wife off his lap and stood up.

"No, I didn't, honey. Really. This couch is more worn-out than we thought," she said. "Now we'll have to get a new one."

"It looks as if you're right, Janet. I guess we'll have to go furniture shopping, but let's look for an inexpensive one. Let's shop carefully, more carefully than we've ever shopped before."

The Parkers go shopping at a discount furniture store. A salesperson meets them at the door.

SALESPERSON: Hi. May I help you today?

JANET: Yes. We're looking for a nice sofa.

SALESPERSON: I'll show you our best.

TED: How about your cheapest?

SALESPERSON: Right here we have the most beautiful sofa in the store. And it's a sleeper. We sell sleepers more frequently than we sell regular sofas. It's on sale now for only twelve hundred dollars. It was originally eighteen hundred.

TED: Twelve hundred dollars! That's too much! May we see something more reasonable?

SALESPERSON: Well, how about this one? It's not very big, but it's only $399.

JANET: Oh, Ted! Come over here! This is just what we need. It's the cutest couch at the best price. And it's so comfortable. See? You sink down into it.

TED: Hey, this is great. I like this one, Janet, but it's a little expensive. It's more than we wanted to pay.

JANET: We can put it on one of our credit cards.

TED: I know, but what about interest? The interest on those cards is so high.

SALESPERSON: No problem. Our store has a payment plan. You can put 10 percent down and pay the rest on time.

JANET: How much would the monthly payments be and for how long would we have to make them?

SALESPERSON: Let's see. Only thirty-eight dollars a month for twenty-four months.

TED: What's the interest on that?

SALESPERSON: It's very reasonable. Only 9.5 percent through our store. The manager has to approve your credit.

TED: What if we want to pay it off early? Is there an early payment penalty?

SALESPERSON: Of course not. There's a penalty only if you miss a payment.

JANET: Let's do it, honey. Let's buy it on time.

TED: Okay. With our good credit, the manager will approve us as soon as he or she can.

Exercises

A.   Answer the questions in complete sentences.

1. What did Janet want?

2. How can Ted sit on their old sofa?

3. How did the legs of the sofa break?

4. How will Ted and Janet buy the new couch?

5. What is their down payment?

6. What will their monthly payments be?

7. When is there a penalty?

8. What does the manager have to do?

B.   Multiple choice   Choose **a, b,** or **c** as the correct answer.

1. The manager has to approve your credit. This means that the manager has to _____ .

   a. tell you how many payments you need to make

   b. tell you your credit is okay

   c. explain the interest to you

2. An extra charge you must pay because you miss a payment is _____ .

   a. a penalty

   b. a deposit

   c. interest

3. When people get upset and begin to use angry words, they are _____ .

   a. settling in

   b. reasonable

   c. arguing

4. Ted didn't want to buy a new sofa. He wouldn't _____ to Janet.

   a. insist

   b. argue

   c. give in

5. Janet said the sofa was worn-out. She meant it was _____ .

   a. broken

   b. inexpensive

   c. old from use

6. Ted thought that Janet had broken the sofa on purpose. This means _____ .

   a. Janet knew what she was doing

   b. Janet sat dow⸗ ⸗oo hard

   c. Janet acci⸗ ⸗ally broke the sofa

7. Ted wanted to look at a more reasonable sofa. This means he didn't want to _____ .

   a. pay interest

   b. buy an expensive couch

   c. buy on time

8. Furniture that is broken in _____ .

   a. is comfortable

   b. is uncomfortable

   c. needs repair

9. The Parkers moved into a little house. They were settled in. This means they _____ .

   a. were moving boxes

   b. were finished putting the house in order

   c. were repairing broken furniture in their new house

10. Ted insisted that the old sofa was comfortable. This means he _____ .

   a. told Janet repeatedly that it was comfortable

   b. would not talk to Janet about the sofa

   c. was able to sit comfortably on the sofa

C. Articles   Complete each sentence with **the** or use an **X** to show that **the** is not necessary. Follow the examples:

   __The__ bumpy sofa in their apartment was worn-out. (specific)

   __X__ bumpy sofas are usually uncomfortable. (in general)

1. _____ interest on those credit cards is very high.

2. They don't like to pay _____ high interest.

3. Ted wanted to look at _____ inexpensive furniture.

4. _____ furniture that the salesman showed them wasn't reasonable.

5. _____ manager of the store has to approve their credit.

6. In general, _____ managers approve credit.

D.   Comparison of adverbs   Complete each sentence with the comparative degree or the comparison of equality of the adverb. Follow the examples:

> You can get credit ___more easily than___ I can.   (easily)
> You'll have credit with the store ___as soon as___ you sign the contract.   (soon)

1. I think you'll sit in this chair _____ on the old sofa. (comfortably)

2. Ted shops _____ Janet.   (carefully)

3. The discount store opens _____ the department store. Let's go there first.   (early)

4. They'd like to pay off the sofa _____ possible. (soon)

5. She shops for clothes _____ she shops for furniture. (frequently)

6. The manager will approve your credit _____ he or she can.   (soon)

E.   Question word order   Make questions by putting the words in the correct order.

1. manager / approve / credit / the / our / Will?

2. make / payments / we / do / many / to / have / How?

3. a / more / May / reasonable / I / see / little / something?

4. penalty / if / pay / we / to / miss / have / a / Do / payment / a / we?

5. the / on / What's / your / interest / store's / plan / payment?

F. **Matching** Read the questions that Ted is asking. Find the salesperson's answers. Write the letter of the correct answer on the line.

<table>
<tr><th>Ted</th><th>Salesperson</th></tr>
<tr><td>_____ 1. May I see something more reasonable?</td><td>a. Only 10 percent down, sir.</td></tr>
<tr><td>_____ 2. It's a little more than I wanted to spend. Can I pay for it on time?</td><td>b. Yes, sir, but the manager must approve your credit.</td></tr>
<tr><td>_____ 3. How much down payment is required?</td><td>c. It's very low. 9.5 percent through our store.</td></tr>
<tr><td>_____ 4. What's the interest?</td><td>d. This is a very popular sleeper. We sell more sleepers than anything else.</td></tr>
<tr><td>_____ 5. What if I want to pay it off early? Is there a penalty?</td><td>e. Of course, sir. Our store has a payment plan.</td></tr>
<tr><td>_____ 6. Okay. May I see the contract?</td><td>f. There's a penalty only if you miss a payment.</td></tr>
</table>

G. **Conversation** How about you?

1. How often do you buy things on time? Why?

2. Do you use credit cards? Why or why not?

3. Tell of a time when you bought furniture or a car on time.

4. Tell of a time when you missed or were late making a payment.

CHAPTER 3

On the Floor?

Vocabulary

appetizer (n)   a small amount of food served before a meal

appreciate (v)   be thankful for

celebration (n)   a party, or other special event, to show happiness

cocktail (n)   an alcoholic drink served before dinner

delightful (adj)   wonderful, marvelous

first-rate (adj)   excellent

spicy (adj)   very hot, as in food; prepared with lots of spices

suggest (v)   mention an idea, advise

unusual (adj)   special, not ordinary, not usual

Idioms

He decided to **talk** it **over** with Janet.   discuss

Janet **gave it some thought**.   thought about it

Ted **made a decision**.   decided

We'll **eat out**.   eat at a restaurant

On the Floor?

Ted wanted to do something special for his boss, Larry Baxter. It was his boss's fiftieth birthday. Larry was a super employer, and Ted appreciated all that his boss was teaching him.

Other employees were planning on getting Larry a shirt or tie or some after-shave, but Ted didn't want to give his boss anything that ordinary. He decided to talk it over with Janet. "Let's get him something unusual, Janet," he said.

"An unusual gift? Well . . . ." Janet gave it some thought. "There's a gift shop at the zoo that sells things from Africa. You could get him an African witch doctor's mask. That's unusual."

"Janet, I want to show my appreciation of him, not scare him. Can't you suggest anything better?" Ted answered.

Janet gave it some more thought.

"I know," she said. "Buy him a dozen roses. Men always give flowers, you know, but they never receive any."

"Are you crazy?" Ted said. "Men don't give men flowers! I'm thankful to the man for all his help, but I'm not in love with him!"

Janet suggested some other gifts, but Ted wasn't able to decide what to buy.

"How about going to a play?" Janet asked. She explained to Ted that there were several excellent plays at the theaters downtown. They talked it over, but Ted couldn't decide what to see.

"A surprise party would be fun," Janet suggested. Ted liked the idea.

"But," he said, "there are so many employees at the office that I wouldn't know whom to invite."

Finally, Ted made a decision. He decided to take Larry and his wife, Joyce, out to dinner.

"We'll eat out," he told Janet. "There's a first-rate Japanese restaurant in town. I understand that all the customers take off their shoes and sit on the floor. It'll be fun. The four of us will be able to enjoy a long, comfortable evening together."

"A comfortable evening, Ted?" Janet asked. "On the floor?"

The two couples, the Baxters and the Parkers, are at the Japanese restaurant. The hostess seats them, and they are now looking at the menu. The waitress comes to their table.

WAITRESS: Good evening. Would anyone like a cocktail?

LARRY: Yes. I'd like to try some sake. How about you, Joyce? Would you like some Japanese rice wine?

JOYCE: That sounds unusual. Yes, I'll try it.

TED: My wife and I will have the same. Make it four.

The waitress leaves to get their drinks.

JANET: Oh, look. There are appetizers and mustard sauce on the table. Would anyone like some?

TED: Be careful of that mustard sauce. It's very spicy. It'll burn your throat.

LARRY: Don't be a chicken, Ted. It's not so spicy. Watch this.

Larry takes a bite of an appetizer covered with mustard sauce. The mustard is so hot that it makes Larry's eyes water.

JOYCE: Larry! Larry! Are you okay? Larry, you're crying.

LARRY: I'm all right. I'm okay. Wow, Ted! You were right. This mustard sauce is hot enough to kill you.

The waitress returns with their sake. She takes their orders. In about twenty minutes, she comes back with their dinners. She tells them to enjoy their meals.

TED: Holy cow! Look at my plate! There's a lot of food here. I don't know if I'll be able to eat it all.

JANET: Are you kidding? I know you can! I cook for you every day.

JOYCE: Everything looks wonderful. It smells delicious. Isn't this delightful? The cook prepared everything delightfully.

LARRY: My sushi looks marvelous. Joyce is right. That Japanese chef prepared everything marvelously.

When everyone is finished eating, the busboy takes away their plates. The waitress returns.

WAITRESS: Would you care for anything else? Some dessert? More sake? More tea?

TED: I don't think so, thank you. None of us are able to eat or drink any more.

The waitress gives Ted the check and leaves. He looks at the bill. It's $99.29. Ted leaves a tip for 15 percent of the total bill. He puts $15.00 on the table for the waitress.

JOYCE: Thank you, Ted and Janet. The dinner was perfect.

LARRY: Yes, it was. You planned my birthday celebration perfectly. I appreciate it.

TED: It's our pleasure, Larry. Happy birthday.

Exercises

A. Answer the questions in complete sentences.

1. Why did Ted want to do something special for his boss?

2. What did Janet suggest first?

3. Why didn't Ted like that idea?

4. What did Janet suggest second?

5. Why didn't Ted like that idea?

6. Where did Ted finally decide to take Larry and Joyce?

7. Where did the customers sit, and what did they do with their shoes?

8. How did the Japanese cook prepare the meals?

9. What did Ted leave for the waitress?

10. What did Joyce say about the dinner?

B. Matching Find the word or phrase in column B that has same meaning as the word or phrase in column A. Write the letter of the correct answer on the line.

	A		**B**
_____	1. appreciate	a.	think about it
_____	2. first-rate	b.	mention an idea
_____	3. delightful	c.	eat at a restaurant
_____	4. give it some thought	d.	discuss
_____	5. unusual	e.	be thankful for
_____	6. make a decision	f.	hot in flavor
_____	7. eat out	g.	not ordinary, special
_____	8. suggest	h.	wonderful, marvelous
_____	9. spicy	i.	excellent
_____	10. talk over	j.	decide

C. Infinitives Complete each sentence with the correct present or past negative response plus the infinitive. Follow the example:

She wanted to buy them an unusual gift, but __she__
__didn't know what to buy__ . (what/buy)

1. They wanted to get her something special, but
   _____ . (what/get)

2. His employees want to give him a wonderful present, but
   _____ . (what/give)

3. Ted thought about taking them to a play, but _____ .
   (where/go)

4. Janet saw many marvelous gifts, but _____ . (which
   one/buy)

5. I'm considering having a party, but _____ .
   (whom/invite)

6. He and his wife discussed going to a restaurant, but
   _____ . (where/dine)

7. We talked about asking some people to our house for dinner,
   but _____ . (whom/ask)

8. They thought about leaving the party, but _____ .
   (when/leave)

9. He wants to go somewhere for his vacation, but
   _____ . (what city/visit)

10. I want to call him about it, but _____ . (when/call)

D. Be able Complete each sentence with the present or past
tense form of the verb **be + able + infinitive**. Follow the
example:

> __Is__ Larry usually __able to eat__
> everything on his plate? (eat)

1. _____ Joyce _____ you yesterday? (help)

2. _____ they always _____ quick decisions? (make)

3. Joyce and Janet _____ their dinners last night. (eat)

4. Ted _____ everything that was on his plate. (finish)

5. I _____ you any time. (help)

6. We _____ to school tomorrow. (not/come)

7. _____ you _____ to their surprise party two weeks ago? (go)

8. They _____ English very well. (speak)

9. _____ you _____ last Sunday? (work)

10. The waitress who served us _____ all the plates at one time. (carry)

E. Adjectives and adverbs Practice these exchanges with a partner. Follow the example:

Marvelous **A:** I think this restaurant is ___marvelous___ .

B: Yes, and they prepare the food ___marvelously___ .

1. Wonderful **A:** Isn't this a _____ dinner?

B: Yes. The cook prepared everything _____ .

2. Perfect **A:** I know of a restaurant that would be _____ for his birthday party.

B: Are you sure? Everything has to be _____ .

A: Oh, yes. At this restaurant they do everything _____ .

3. Good

A: Sushi? That sounds _____ . I'll have that.

B: Me, too. The sushi here is made quite

_____ .

4. Terrible

A: He's (She's) a _____ dancer. I don't want to dance with him (her).

B: Me, neither. He (She) dances _____ .

5. Careful

A: We aren't in a hurry. Please slow down and drive _____ .

B: I always drive _____ . I'm a very _____ driver.

6. Bad

A: Oh! I cut myself with this knife. It looks

_____ .

B: Yes, it does. I think you cut yourself very

_____ .

7. Delightful

A: Wow! Look at this _____ birthday gift!

B: Yes, and she wrapped it in such _____ paper. She wrapped it _____ .

8. Easy   **A:** If you want to see her, you can
                  _____ catch her at the office before
                  5:00 P.M.

               B: That sounds _____ . I'll try to
                  catch her right now.

F.   Restaurant ordering   You are in a restaurant. Complete the
dialogue with a partner.

WAITRESS: Are you ready to order?

CUSTOMER: Yes. I'd like _____ .

WAITRESS: Would you like _____ with your meal?

CUSTOMER: Oh, no. I never _____ .

The waitress takes the customer's order and returns later with
his or her plate.

WAITRESS: Be careful. The plate _____ . I hope
            _____ .

CUSTOMER: Thank you. Everything _____ .

WAITRESS: Can I get you _____ ?

CUSTOMER: No, _____ .

The waitress leaves. She returns in a little while.

WAITRESS: May I take _____ ?

CUSTOMER: Yes, I'm _____ .

On the Floor? **33**

WAITRESS: How ——————— ?

CUSTOMER: Everything ——————— .

WAITRESS: Would you ——————— ?

CUSTOMER: I don't think so. Just the ———————, please.

WAITRESS: Here ——————— . And I hope you'll
——————— .

CUSTOMER: I will. I'll be back ——————— .

G. Conversation How about you?

1. How often do you eat out? Why? Where do you go?

2. What are some of the things that you like about eating at a restaurant? How about some of the things you don't like?

3. Explain why a waiter or waitress almost always receives a tip. Explain why he or she sometimes doesn't.

4. Did you ever have bad service at a restaurant? What happened?

5. Do you like to eat at fast-food restaurants? Why or why not?

CHAPTER 4

With You Alone

Vocabulary

first-class (adj)   the best, the most expensive

huge (adj)   very big

promotion (n)   advancement in a job, a better position

raise (n)   higher pay

reconfirm (v)   call back to make sure of an appointment or reservation

reservation (n)   a place saved for a person

rush (v)   hurry

shocked (adj)   very surprised

significant (adj)   important

takeoff (n)   departure of a plane

vacant (adj)   available, free to use

Idioms

Let's **order out.**   order a meal from a restaurant for pickup or delivery

We're **all set** for San Francisco.   ready

You **are booked** on Flight 568.   have a reservation

With You Alone

Ted got a promotion from his boss. The boss gave it to him last Friday afternoon. He also gave Ted a huge raise. The boss gave it to him that same day.

Ted rushed home to tell Janet the news. Janet was so shocked that she almost fell on the floor.

"I can't believe it, Ted," she said. "A promotion and a huge raise! That's great, honey. How should we celebrate? I know. I'll cook a complete Mexican dinner. We'll have tacos and beans and rice and everything!"

Ted didn't want Janet to spend a lot of time in the kitchen.

"Let's order out," he suggested. "We'll get some take-out food. How about Chinese? And I'll pick up a bottle of champagne. We can't celebrate without champagne!"

While Ted was gone, Janet set the table and got out some candles. She changed into a pretty dress and put on perfume. When Ted returned, they had a romantic dinner by candlelight.

"You know, Janet," Ted said, "the advancement that Larry gave me is a very significant one. And the raise is unbelievable. I think we should celebrate our good luck by taking a weekend trip. How about it?"

Janet was surprised. "Really? A weekend trip? Of course, I'd love it! We could go to the mountains or to the beach, or we could visit my family."

Ted almost choked on an egg roll. "Visit your family! No way! I want to celebrate with you alone!"

"Okay," Janet said. "You know, we've always wanted to see San Francisco, Ted."

"Then San Francisco it is, Janet. I'll make the flight reservations tomorrow."

The next day Ted gets on the telephone to make airline reservations for San Francisco. Janet wants to hear his

36

conversation with the airline representative, so she moves close to Ted and puts her ear by the telephone receiver.

TED: Hello. I'd like to make a reservation for two to San Francisco.

AGENT: On what date, sir?

TED: Next Friday, the twenty-third. Is there a flight leaving in the late afternoon?

AGENT: I have a flight leaving on the twenty-third at 4:14 P.M., but there are only first-class seats available.

JANET: What did he say? First class? That's good, Ted. I like first class.

TED: Janet, please! I can't hear! Don't you have any seats available in tourist class?

AGENT: Not on that flight, sir. I have two seats available in tourist class on a flight leaving a little earlier that day. It departs at 3:26 P.M.

JANET: What, Ted? Did he say 3:26? That's okay. It's not too early. We can make it. Tell him it's okay.

TED: Sh! Janet, I can't hear. That'll be fine. We'll take the 3:26 P.M. flight. The last name is Parker. That's spelled P-A-R-K-E-R. The first name is Ted.

AGENT: All right, sir. You are booked on Flight 568, departing San Diego at 3:26 P.M. and arriving in San Francisco at 4:37 P.M. Please call back twenty-four hours before your departure time to reconfirm your reservations. Check in at the airline desk one hour before takeoff.

TED: I'll remember to reconfirm. Thank you. There, honey. We're all set for San Francisco.

JANET: All set? Are you sure, Ted?

TED: Of course I'm sure. We're all set to fly out Friday afternoon.

JANET: But, Ted, how about hotel reservations? You don't want to sleep on a park bench, do you?

Exercises

A.   Answer the questions in complete sentences.

1. What two things did the boss give Ted?

2. How did Janet feel about the good news?

3. What did Janet want to do for Ted?

4. How did Ted want to celebrate that evening?

5. Why didn't Ted want to visit Janet's family?

6. Who did Ted talk to for airline reservations?

7. What kind of seats on the plane did Ted want?

8. What was the problem with the 4:14 P.M. flight?

9. What did the agent tell Ted to do twenty-four hours before takeoff?

10. When did they need to check in at the airline desk?

B. **Take one out** Read each of the word groups. Take out the word that does not belong.

1. significant, important, celebrate, terrific

2. run, reconfirm, rush, hurry

3. fantastic, unbelievable, super, shocked

4. difficult, huge, large, big

5. reservation, promotion, advancement, raise

6. agent, airline, employee, representative

7. available, vacant, first-class, ready

8. take off, check in, leave, depart

C. **Objects** Change each sentence so that the indirect object becomes the object of the preposition. Follow the example:

The boss gave __him__ a raise. (to)
The boss gave a raise __to him__ .

1. Ted ordered her some Chinese food. (for)

2. The agent is giving them seats on Flight 568. (to)

3. His wife wanted to make him a huge dinner. (for)

4. The manager showed me his huge new office. (to)

5. She handed us the tickets. (to)

6. I already told you the good news. (to)

7. The flight hostess showed us the airsickness bags. (to)

8. He's going to give the airline representative four hundred dollars. (to)

9. The owner of the company offered Ted a promotion. (to)

10. The waiter brought them some champagne. (for)

D. Objects   Change each sentence so that the object of the preposition becomes the indirect object. Follow the example:

> The boss gave a raise <u>to him</u> . (him)
> The boss gave <u>him</u> a raise.

1. The Parkers are going to show their vacation pictures to the boss. (the boss)

2. The agent gave the wrong tickets to them. (them)

3. The company has offered a better job to me. (me)

4. Mr. Parker handed an egg roll to his wife. (his wife)

5. Janet sent a postcard to her parents. (her parents)

6. The hotel desk clerk brought the room key to them. (them)

7. We'll make a huge dinner for the family. (the family)

8. I'll tell the story to you later. (you)

9. Could you make dinner for me? (me)

10. Janet gave a big kiss to Ted. (Ted)

E.   Adjective clauses   Use **that** to combine the pairs of sentences. Follow the example:

The promotion was unbelievable. He gave me the promotion.
The promotion __that he gave me__ was unbelievable.

1. The flight was canceled. They wanted the flight.

2. The raise is huge. The boss is giving me the raise.

3. The Chinese food tasted terrific. Ted ordered the Chinese food.

4. The vacation will be fantastic. I'm going to take the vacation.

5. The reservation was for Flight 568. The agent gave me the reservation.

6. The seats were not available. We wanted the seats.

7. The flight was full. Ted wanted to take the flight.

8. The city has many nice restaurants. They want to visit the city.

9. The job pays a lot of money. Ted got the job.

10. The raise helped solve their money problems. The boss gave him the raise.

F. Hotel reservation   You are a guest at this hotel. Practice asking and answering these questions with a partner. Answer in complete sentences.

CLERK: Welcome to Hotel Gotrocks. How may I help you?

GUEST: (Say that you have a reservation. Give your name.)

CLERK: Oh, yes. I have your reservation here. That's for a double room, isn't it?

GUEST: Yes. (Say that you and your wife/husband/friend are planning to stay for two nights.)

CLERK: Could you spell the last name, please?

GUEST: (Spell your last name.)

CLERK: Please register here. I need your name, address, make of car, license plate number, and driver's license number.

GUEST: (Ask if the hotel has a gift shop and room service.)

CLERK: Yes, sir (ma'am). Our hotel has everything. If you have any questions, feel free to ask me. I'm here to help.

GUEST: (Say that you're sure you're going to enjoy your stay here. Say thanks.)

G.   **Conversation**   How about you?

1. How often do employees usually get raises? How about you?

2. How often do most people take a trip? How about you? Why?

3. Think of your next vacation. Where do you want to go? What do you want to do?

4. Do you ever fly? Where do you go? Why? Do you get airsick?

5. Tell about your best vacation.

6. Tell about your worst vacation.

7. What are some reasons that people stay at home during their vacations?

CHAPTER 5

It Must Be Inflation

Vocabulary

amount (n)	total in money or numbers
budget (n)	a list of income and expenses
entertainment (n)	fun, play
expenses (n)	payments and bills
groceries (n)	food and other household products a person buys at the supermarket
income (n)	money a person makes on the job
inflation (n)	rising prices

Idioms

Those football tickets **cost an arm and a leg**.	are expensive
We're going to have to **cut down** on our spending.	lower, reduce
I'll **cut out** going to football games.	eliminate, omit
We'll have to **do without** air conditioning.	live day to day without a certain item
Ted **figured out** how much money he and his wife brought home.	calculated, solved
In addition, they calculated how much money they needed.	also
Prices **kept getting** higher.	continued
We have to **take the bull by the horns**.	take control
Every penny counts.	every little way to save money is helpful

It Must Be Inflation

"Janet, we're going to have to cut down on our spending," Ted told his wife one evening while he was writing out checks to pay bills. "We used to save money each month, but we don't anymore. I don't know how it happened, but each month we spend more and more money."

"It must be inflation," Janet said. "The cost of things used to be cheaper. Prices keep getting higher, especially food and gas. And don't forget that the landlady raised our rent not too long ago."

"That's true," Ted answered. "But we have to take the bull by the horns and do something about it. We should really sit down and compare our monthly income with our monthly expenses. Let's start a budget. Right now."

First, they made a list of all their expenses. They paid rent, car payments on Ted's car, the gas bill, the electric bill, the phone bill, the cable TV bill, and credit card bills. In addition, they calculated how much money they needed each month for groceries, clothing, toiletries and cosmetics, gasoline, and entertainment. The amount was much higher than they thought it would be.

Next, Ted figured out how much money he and his wife brought home each month. He saw that their income couldn't cover the total amount of their expenses. It was time to cut down.

Ted and Janet are sitting at the dining table trying to find a way to cut down on their expenses and save money.

TED: One of our biggest problems is credit card bills.

JANET: Oh, I didn't charge too many things last month, did I?

TED: Not just you. Me, too. It's so easy to take out that piece of plastic and charge things. We'll have to be more careful, won't we?

JANET: I guess so. I won't charge gasoline anymore. It's cheaper to pay cash.

TED: That'll help. We should cut down on our entertainment costs, too, shouldn't we? We go out a lot, probably too much—movies, dancing, restaurants. I used to go to a lot of football games, but I'll cut out going to the games. Those football tickets cost an arm and a leg. What about you, Janet? You don't have to go to that beauty salon all the time, do you?

JANET: I guess not. I used to get my hair cut there every month, but I'll try to cut my own hair. I'll cut yours, too. Every penny counts. What else?

TED: We used to take the cars to the car wash, but I'll start washing the cars here at home.

JANET: We can save a lot of money on groceries, can't we? We'll be sure to check the price of every item, and I'll start saving more coupons. Every penny counts.

TED: We'll also have to forget about buying any new clothes for a while.

JANET: Forget about new clothes? You don't mean new shoes, too, do you?

TED: Oh, Janet! You don't need any new shoes! You have enough shoes in your closet to open your own shoe store.

JANET: I do not! Be nice to me, Ted. I'll try very hard not to buy any new shoes. Now, what else can we do to cut down on our expenses?

TED: We used to turn on the air conditioner in the summertime. We'll have to do without air conditioning. In addition, we'll have to do without heat in the wintertime. At night, anyway.

JANET: No heat? We'll freeze!

TED: Honey, I wouldn't let you freeze, would I? In the evening we can turn on the electric blanket and watch TV in bed.

Exercises

A.   Answer the questions in complete sentences.

1. What keeps happening to prices because of inflation?

2. What are Ted and Janet going to start?

3. What list did they make first?

4. What was wrong with their income?

5. What was one of their biggest money problems?

6. What was the problem with Ted's football tickets?

7. What will Janet try to do with her own hair?

8. What did they decide to do in the summertime and in the wintertime?

B.   **Multiple choice**   Choose **a, b,** or **c** as the correct answer.

1. Ted said that football tickets cost an arm and a leg. This means that _____ .

    a. the tickets were very expensive

    b. the tickets were difficult to get

    c. many football players break arms and legs

2. Janet wants to cut Ted's hair, too, because every penny counts. This means that _____ .

    a. Janet is counting the change in her wallet

    b. every little way to save money helps

    c. Ted would pay her a little for cutting his hair

3. Ted figured out how much money they brought home each month. This means that _____ .

    a. Ted worked well with numbers

    b. Ted calculated their monthly income

    c. Ted wanted to start the budget

4. Ted and Janet learned that their income couldn't cover the total amount of their expenses. This means that _____ .

    a. Janet worked only a short time

    b. they wanted to make a short budget

    c. the income they brought home was not enough to pay for their expenses

5. Janet said, "Prices keep getting higher." This means that _____ .

    a. she doesn't like inflation

    b. costs continue to rise

    c. groceries are very expensive

6. Ted said, "We have to take the bull by the horns." This means that _____ .

    a. Ted and Janet are going to get a bull for beef

    b. Ted decided to become a bullfighter

    c. Ted wants to take control of their money problems

7. Ted told Janet, "We'll have to do without heat." This means that _____ .

    a. they won't turn on the heat in the wintertime

    b. they won't freeze in the wintertime

    c. they'll have to forget the air conditioning

8. Ted and Janet made a list of their expenses. In addition, they calculated their income. **In addition** means _____ .

    a. Ted is adding all of their expenses

    b. also

    c. the total amount

9. The Parkers have to cut down on spending. This means that _____ .

    a. they're going to cut coupons out of the newspaper

    b. they have to throw away their credit cards

    c. they have to spend less money each month

10. Ted decided to cut out going to his football games. This means that _____ .

    a. Ted cut himself at the game

    b. Ted is going to stop going to football games

    c. Ted will not go to so many football games

C. Tag questions Complete each sentence with the correct tag question. Use a helping verb and a pronoun. Follow the example:

You don't need a haircut, <u>do you</u> ?

1. They won't spend too much money, _____ ?

2. I can't go to the football games anymore, _____ ?

3. She doesn't buy very many shoes now, _____ ?

4. The Parkers aren't turning on the heat, _____ ?

5. You don't understand me, _____ ?

6. We shouldn't go out so much anymore, _____ ?

7. Ted didn't figure out the budget, _____ ?

8. She didn't pay the rent this month, _____ ?

9. He wasn't saving any money, _____ ?

10. It wasn't freezing, _____ ?

D.   Tag questions   Complete each sentence with the correct tag question. Use a helping verb and a pronoun. Follow the example:

You need a haircut, __don't you__ ?

1. Ted and Janet made a budget, _____ ?

2. It's a big problem, _____ ?

3. She'll probably buy more shoes, _____ ?

4. He was going to a football game, _____ ?

5. She has a million shoes in her closet, _____ ?

6. They stopped using their credit cards, _____ ?

7. We were spending too much, _____ ?

8. I should cut down on my expenses, _____ ?

9. Janet cut his hair last week, _____ ?

10. Ted's going to take the bull by the horns, _____ ?

E.   Used to   Practice these exchanges with a partner.
Complete each sentence with the idiom **used to** and the correct
verb. Follow the example:

   A: I thought he always took the bus to school.

   B: He ___used to take___ the bus, but now he
      walks. (take)

1. **A:** I thought he always played football on Sundays.

   B: He _____ football, but now he plays soccer.
      (play)

2. **A:** I thought they always paid their bills in cash.

   B: They _____ their bills in cash, but now they pay
      by check. (pay)

3. **A:** I heard that she always got her hair cut at the beauty
      salon.

   B: She _____ her hair cut there, but now she cuts
      her own hair.   (get)

4. **A:** I understand you always sleep late on Saturday mornings.

   B: I _____ late on Saturdays, but now I have to get
      up early. (sleep)

5. **A:** I thought you always saved your extra money.

   B: I _____ it, but I have a girlfriend (boyfriend) now.
      (save)

6. **A:** I understand that the Parkers go out a lot.

   B: They _____ out often, but now they stay home.
   (go)

7. **A:** I heard that the price of gas was going up again.

   B: Yes. Gas _____ cheap, but now it's expensive.
   (be)

8. **A:** I thought that they lived on Elm Street.

   B: They _____ on Elm, but now they live on Fig.
   (live)

G. **Conversation** How about you?

1. Do you have any money problems? How can you help yourself?

2. Do you spend a lot of money on entertainment?

3. How do you usually spend your extra cash?

4. How can you lower your gas bill and your electric bill?

5. Tell of a time when you had to cut out doing something because it was too expensive.

F. **The budget**   Use the list to make a budget for yourself.

Monthly Expenses

Rent	$_____
Phone	$_____
Gas/Electric	$_____
Car payment	$_____
Cable TV	$_____
Food	$_____
Clothes	$_____
Gasoline	$_____
Toiletries	$_____
Entertainment	$_____
Other	$_____
Other	$_____
Other	$_____
TOTAL	$_____

Compare with monthly income $_____

CHAPTER 6

It's Not Enough

Vocabulary

deduct (v)	take money out of a paycheck
dues (n)	monthly payment to a labor union
federal (adj)	of the central government, of the U.S. government
FICA (n)	Social Security tax, Federal Insurance Contribution Act
gross pay (n)	pay (income) before deductions
net pay (n)	income after deductions, take-home pay
pay stub (n)	part of a paycheck kept as a record
union (n)	labor organization that fights for employees' rights and benefits
withholding tax (n)	tax deducted for the federal government

Idioms

We're **sticking to** our budget.	continuing something
They were still **strapped for money**.	in need of money
We have trouble **making ends meet**.	having an income large enough to pay the bills
Every month we **end up** without any cash in the bank.	result, come to an end
We have to **get out of** this mess.	get free of
We're already living on the **bare necessities**.	the things needed to live day to day

It's Not Enough

Ted and Janet planned their budget carefully and they stuck to it, but they found that they were still strapped for money.

TED: It's incredible, Janet, that we have trouble making ends meet. Wouldn't you think that we could save some money? But at the end of every month we end up without any cash in the bank. Something's wrong, Janet. We have to think of a way to get ourselves out of this mess.

JANET: Why can't we cut down some more? Cut out more spending?

TED: We're already living on the bare necessities. Didn't we cut out entertainment and eating out and sporting events?

JANET: Well, yes, except for our trip to San Francisco. We put everything on our credit cards. Now the bills are coming in. The flight, the hotel, dinners in Chinatown, gifts for the family, and the concert. It was an expensive trip, Ted.

TED: And let's not forget that new sofa. A sleeper sofa!

JANET: Why don't we borrow money from my mother? Then we could pay off the sofa and get out of one bill.

TED: Oh, Janet. I don't want to borrow money from your mother. Then we'd have to pay her back instead of the store. It's all the same. Why shouldn't I get a second job? I could work evenings and weekends.

JANET: You can't work a full-time job during the day and a part-time job nights and weekends. You'd kill yourself!

TED: I don't understand it. We're sticking to our budget and watching every penny, but still we're strapped for money.

JANET: Well, let's examine our pay stubs. You make good money, and I bring home pay from my part-time job, but it's not enough. Let's see why.

Ted and Janet got their pay stubs for the last pay periods and looked them over. They found that a lot of money had to be deducted from their paychecks every pay period.

"This is incredible," Ted said. "Look at our deductions! This is terrible."

Their companies had to deduct withholding tax for the federal government, state tax for the state of California, and FICA for social security. Also, Ted's company made a large deduction for medical and dental insurance for him and Janet. Janet had to pay union dues. It ended up that their take-home pay was much smaller than their pay before deductions.

"Look at my pay stub," Ted said. "I can't believe it. Withholding tax, $140.31; state tax, $58.92; FICA, $85.70. And look at that big deduction the company has to take for insurance. Now I see why we can't make ends meet. My net pay is next to nothing."

Janet showed her pay stub to Ted. "Mine isn't any better, honey. My deductions are high, too. Taxes, taxes, taxes! How can anybody save any money? It's impossible. And look at my union dues. They're too high. I only work part-time."

Ted thought that Janet's job was more of a problem than a help. He said, "Janet, you're not making a very good hourly wage at that job, and you have to pay heavy union dues. I don't think your part-time job is helping us very much."

"Well," Janet decided, "I'll go out and look for a good full-time job. I have experience with computers, and I'm a terrific employee. Any company would be happy to get me. I'll start looking tomorrow afternoon, Ted. I'll work full-time. That's our answer, Ted. That's our answer."

Exercises

A.   Answer the questions in complete sentences.

1. What trouble were Ted and Janet having?

2. What did they already cut out?

3. How did Janet want to pay off the sofa?

4. What did Ted want to do to make more money?

5. What did they look over?

6. What deductions were deducted from Ted's paycheck?

7. Why was Janet upset about her union dues?

8. What did Janet decide to do?

B.   **True or false**   Read each sentence. Write **T** on the line if
the sentence is true. Write **F** on the line if it is false.

_____   1. If you're strapped for money, you have enough money
to go out to dinner.

_____   2. Withholding tax is tax that goes to the federal
government.

_____   3. FICA is state tax.

_____   4. Gross pay is pay after deductions, your take-home
pay.

_____   5. If you pay union dues, you pay money to the union
every month in order to belong to that union.

_____ 6. Withholding tax is an example of a deduction.

_____ 7. If you stick to your job, you quit.

_____ 8. If you live on the bare necessities, you don't spend any money on entertainment.

_____ 9. Your pay stub shows you your gross pay, but not your net pay.

_____ 10. If you can't make ends meet, you probably can't pay all of your monthly bills.

_____ 11. The federal government is the U.S. government.

_____ 12. If you want to free yourself of a problem, you want to get out of it.

C. Negative questions Make negative questions. Begin each question with **Why.** Follow the example:

We can save money.

Why can't we save money?

1. They could borrow money from her mother.

2. He'll look for a full-time job.

3. You should get a second job. (I)

4. They're making ends meet.

5. The Parkers paid off the sofa.

6. I pay union dues. (you)

7. The company deducts for insurance.

8. They were putting money into the bank.

9. The Parkers lived on the bare necessities.

10. She was sticking to her budget.

D.   Have to   Complete each sentence with the present, past, or future form of **have to** and the verb. Follow the example:

I ___have to put___ money in the bank.   (put)

1. She _____ a full-time job.   (get)

2. Last year, I _____ a lot of taxes.   (pay)

3. In the future, we _____ to our budget.   (stick)

4. Everyone in the company _____ the union.   (join)

5. You _____ ends meet if you want to pay all your bills.
   (make)

6. Next year, I _____ out spending so much money on
   entertainment.   (cut)

7. The company _____ money for FICA from every
   paycheck.   (deduct)

8. We _____ on the bare necessities last year.   (live)

9. The Parkers _____ their pay stubs last week.
   (examine)

10. We _____ out of this mess next month.   (get)

E. Have to   Change the sentences to questions. Follow the example:

They had to make ends meet.

Did they have to make ends meet?

1. The company has to deduct for FICA.

2. Janet has to pay union dues.

3. I had to look at my pay stub. (you)

4. Ted will have to stick to the budget.

5. The boss had to explain the deductions.

F. Have to   Change each sentence to the negative form. Follow the example:

Ted has to get dental insurance.

Ted doesn't have to get dental insurance.

1. I'll have to talk to you later.

2. She has to look for another job.

3. Ted and Janet had to cut out sporting events.

4. The company had to deduct union dues.

5. We have to pay it off right away.

G.   Read the pay stub and answer the questions in complete sentences.

Capital Business Machines				Retain for your records		
Employee Name		**Social Security No.**		**Period Ending**		**Marital Status**
SCHWARTZ, JOHN		006-00-0034		11/15/90		M
Earnings				**Deductions**		
Class	Hours	Rate	Amount	Description		Amount
Reg.	80H	8.75	700.00	W/H TX		74.36
OT	6H	13.13	78.78	ST TX		14.60
				FICA		59.80
				Group Ins.		64.21
Total Gross Pay			778.78	**Total Deductions**		212.97
		Total Net Pay	565.81			

1. What is the employee's last name?

2. What is his social security number?

3. Is he married or single?

4. How many hours of overtime did he work?

5. How much does he make for overtime pay?

6. What is his regular hourly wage?

7. How much money did they deduct from his paycheck?

8. How much money did they take out for social security?

9. How much money did they take out for federal income tax?

10. What did he pay $14.60 for?

11. How many weeks did he work for this paycheck?

12. What is his take-home pay?

H. Conversation   How about you?

1. Do you have a job? Is your job part-time or full-time?

2. Do you look carefully at each of your pay stubs? Why or why not?

3. Do you belong to a union?

CHAPTER 7

A Good Catch

Vocabulary

anxious (adj)	nervous
benefits (n)	what the company gives an employee in addition to pay
category (n)	classification, group
field (n)	area of experience or training
fired (adj)	told by the boss to leave the job
job request form (n)	form to fill out at the state employment office for a job
lay off (v)	dismiss from a job temporarily
notice (n)	job announcement
printout (n)	list of information from a computer
quit (v)	leave a job
salary (n)	pay, wages
unemployment insurance (n)	money received by a person who is temporarily unemployed

Idioms

Calm down, Janet Parker.	Take it easy.
I'm going to **set up** interviews for you.	prepare, arrange
Janet **filled out** three job request forms.	completed (a form)
You'll need to **fill in** your name.	complete (a blank)

A Good Catch

Janet was feeling very anxious as she walked through the parking lot of the state employment office. She didn't want to look nervous, so she took a deep breath and talked to herself.

"These people are here to help you. Calm down and take it easy, Janet Parker!"

She entered the building and saw people standing in a very long line. A young woman was waiting in line when Janet walked up to her and said, "Excuse me. What's this line for?"

The woman began explaining that the line was for people who wanted to apply for unemployment insurance. "You know, people are laid off or fired, or they quit. Then they apply for unemployment insurance so they can collect some money while they're looking for another job. I was working at a sewing shop when they laid me off. I have to pay the bills, you know?"

"Yes, I see. Thank you," said Janet. That was not the line she needed.

Luckily, Janet saw a sign marked **Information.** The clerk was completing a form when Janet walked up to his window. She asked him for help in finding a full-time job.

"Do you see all of those job notices on the bulletin boards over there?" The employee was pointing out hundreds of computer printouts on bulletin boards hanging on the walls. "Those are the job openings we have. Take a look at them."

The clerk told Janet that each printout had lists of different jobs available in different job categories. There were jobs available in computers, landscaping, construction, sales, clerical services, and professions.

"If you see a job or two that you're interested in," he explained, "get some job request forms and fill them out. You'll need to fill in your name and social security number, the job titles, and the job numbers. When you're done filling out the job requests, put them in the basket on the counter, take a seat, and wait for someone to call your name. It doesn't take too long."

"Oh, thank you," Janet said. She felt excited at seeing so many job notices on the boards. She wanted a job that paid a good salary and also gave her some benefits.

Janet filled out three job request forms, put them in the correct basket, and sat down to wait.

After about twenty minutes, Janet hears her name called. A woman has Janet's three job request forms in her hand. Janet follows the woman to her desk.

MS. LYNCH: Hello. My name's Dorothy Lynch. May I call you Janet?

JANET: Of course.

MS. LYNCH: I see that you're interested in computer programming. Do you have any experience?

JANET: Yes. I worked on the computers in the registration office at the junior college I was attending.

MS. LYNCH: I see. How long did you work in the registration office?

JANET: Eight months. I have my programmer's certificate from the college, too.

MS. LYNCH: That's good. Why did you leave that job?

JANET: I was laid off. They always lay off workers in the summer. They weren't sure if they were going to call me back, so I took a job in computer sales. Right now I work part-time as an instructor's aide in computer classes at a high school here in San Diego.

MS. LYNCH: I understand. And what about shifts? What shift would you prefer to work?

JANET: I'd enjoy working days, but I'm available for any shift.

MS. LYNCH: Good. And do you have transportation?

JANET: Yes, I do. I have a car.

MS. LYNCH: Well, Janet, you look like a good catch for some fine company. I'm going to contact these three companies and set up interviews for you. When's the best time for you to go to an interview?

JANET: I work mornings, so afternoons would be best, but I'd consider interviewing in the morning. I can make myself available.

MS. LYNCH: Great, Janet! I'll be calling you at home as soon as I have interview times. It was a pleasure talking to you. And good luck in your career.

JANET: Thank you, Ms. Lynch. You're very helpful.

Exercises

A.   Answer the questions in complete sentences.

1. Why did Janet take a deep breath and talk to herself?

2. Janet entered the building and saw a long line. What was the line for?

3. What is unemployment insurance?

4. Where were the job notices?

5. What forms did Janet have to fill out?

6. When she was done filling out the forms, what did she have to do?

7. Where did Janet get her computer experience?

8. What shift is Janet available for?

9. What time would be best for Janet to interview?

10. When will Ms. Lynch be calling Janet?

B.   **Multiple choice**   Choose a, b, or c as the correct answer.

1. The manager told some of the employees that they couldn't work during the summer. He said that he'd call them back to work in the fall. He _____ these employees.

   a. fired

   b. laid off

   c. hired

2. You are looking for a job at the state employment office. You see a job that you'd like to apply for. You need to fill out a job _____ .

   a. bulletin

   b. category

   c. request form

3. The computer makes copies of information. The employees at the state employment office put these copies on the bulletin boards. These computer copies are _____ .

   a. printouts

   b. requests

   c. categories

4. Clerical, professional, and construction are examples of job _____ .

   a. salaries

   b. unemployment insurance

   c. categories

5. Ms. Lynch was going to set up interviews for Janet. This means that Ms. Lynch _____ .

   a. was going to make appointments for Janet to have interviews

   b. wanted Janet to tell her what shift she preferred working

   c. needed to get more information on Janet before the interviews

6. Janet was feeling anxious as she walked into the employment office. This means that she was feeling _____ .

   a. calmed down

   b. nervous

   c. excited

7. I'm at the state employment office and I'm reading about different jobs available in the clerical field. I'm reading

   _____ .

   a. the job notices

   b. the request forms

   c. all of the job categories

8. Paid vacation, paid holidays, and paid medical insurance are examples of _____ .

   a. unemployment insurance

   b. benefits

   c. notices

9. You write your name and social security number on the lines. You _____ the blanks.

   a. fill in

   b. fill out

   c. set up

10. You completed an application. You _____ the application.

   a. filled in

   b. filled out

   c. set up

C. Gerunds Complete each sentence with the gerund form of the word in parentheses. Follow the example:

> The woman began __explaining__ that the line was for people who wanted unemployment insurance. (explain)

1. I'm interested in _____ full-time. (work)

2. Janet felt excited at _____ so many job notices. (see)

3. Would you prefer _____ or _____ ? (program)(landscape)

4. I'd consider _____ in the morning. (interview)

5. Ms. Lynch wasn't interested in _____ about her personal problems. (hear)

6. Do you think you'd enjoy _____ in an office? (work)

7. The unemployed people began _____ out job request forms. (fill)

8. Would you consider _____ to the night shift? (change)

9. Most people don't enjoy _____ laid off. (get)

10. Janet wanted help in _____ a full-time job. (find)

D. Past/past continuous   Complete each sentence with either the past tense or the past continuous tense. Follow the example:

> Janet __was feeling__ very anxious as she
> __walked__ into the state employment office.
> (feel)(walk)

1. The woman _____ in line when Janet _____ her what the line was for. (wait) (ask)

2. The clerk _____ out the bulletin boards as he _____ to Janet. (point) (talk)

3. She _____ and _____ when she _____ her name called. (sit) (wait) (hear)

4. She _____ a deep breath and _____ to herself because she _____ to calm down. (take) (talk) (try)

5. Janet _____ with Ms. Lynch when the phone _____ . (speak) (ring)

6. The people _____ in line because they _____ unemployment insurance. (stand) (want)

7. She _____ at a part-time job when she _____ to look for a full-time job. (work) (decide)

8. When the clerk _____ their names, they _____ at the job notices. (call) (look)

9. When she _____ laid off, she _____ at a sewing shop. (get) (work)

10. When she _____ up to the employee's window, he _____ a form. (walk) (complete)

E. Job categories   Choose the correct category for each job. Write the letter of the correct answer on the line.

Categories: **a.** Landscaping
b. Construction
c. Sales
d. Clerical
e. Professional

_____ 1. Tree planter

_____ 2. Nurse

_____ 3. Carpenter

_____ 4. Yard worker

_____ 5. Bookkeeper

_____ 6. Shoe clerk

_____ 7. Teacher's aide

_____ 8. Receptionist

_____ 9. High school registrar

_____ 10. Sprinkler installer

_____ 11. Lawyer

_____ 12. Computer sales representative

_____ 13. Secretary

_____ 14. Phone solicitor

_____ 15. Dry-waller

F.   **Conversation**   How about you?

1. How do you usually find work?

2. Did you ever go without work? What did you do?

3. How many ways can you find out about job openings?

4. Why do you think there is unemployment insurance?

5. Would you like to look for another job? Why or why not?

6. Do you think you could find a better job? Why or why not?

CHAPTER 8

What This Independent Woman Needs

Vocabulary

balance (n)   the amount of money in a checking account or savings account

deposit (v)   put money into the bank

duties (n)   chores, responsibilities

expect (v)   believe something will happen

joint (adj)   together, joined

minimum (adj)   the least, the smallest amount

personalized (adj)   printed with one's name and address

quite (adv)   really, very

relaxation (n)   rest, recreation

signature card (n)   a card one fills out before getting an account

Idioms

I need you to **pitch in,** Ted.   contribute, help

Ted was **getting** his golf clubs **together.**   gathering, uniting

Don't **fly off the handle** at me, Janet.   get angry

What happens if I **fall below the minimun balance?**   fail to keep a certain amount of money in an account

I **would rather** have an individual account.   prefer

You **had better** pick the checks you like.   should

What This Independent Woman Needs

Now that Janet was working full-time as a computer programmer, she was making very good money. She felt quite proud of herself, and she wanted some changes around the house.

When Janet was working only part-time, she was able to take care of the household duties, but now that she was working full-time, she expected her husband to contribute to the regular chores.

"I need you to pitch in, Ted," she informed her husband one Saturday morning. Janet was gathering dirty clothes to start the laundry. Ted was getting his golf clubs together for his regular Saturday morning golf date with a friend.

"I'm working full-time now, but I still end up shopping and cleaning and washing and cooking," she said. "Here we are on a Saturday morning—I'm getting ready for laundry and you're getting ready for golf. It isn't fair, Ted." Janet was a little angry at her husband.

"Don't fly off the handle at me, Janet," Ted answered. "I work hard all week long, Monday through Friday. I need to go golfing for some relaxation. I don't want to think about laundry." Ted was a little angry at his wife.

Janet informed Ted that she, too, worked hard all week and that she, too, would like to go somewhere for some relaxation. She told him that doing laundry was not her idea of fun.

"Then don't do the laundry," Ted told her as he picked up his golf bag to leave the house. "This is a free country, Janet, and you're an independent woman with a good-paying, full-time job. You don't have to do the laundry if you don't want to." Ted walked out of the house, closed the door behind him, and drove away for his golf date.

Janet stood in the living room with her mouth open. She was quite surprised by Ted's answer, but after thinking about it, she decided that he was right. She didn't want to do laundry. Janet dropped the laundry basket in the middle of the living room floor.

"Ted's right," she told herself. "I am independent, and what this independent woman needs is her very own checking account for her very own money!"

Janet left the house to go to a bank. The laundry basket stayed on the living room floor.

Janet is at a bank. She's talking to Dee Johnson, an employee who is helping her with her new account.

JANET: I'm interested in opening a checking account. May I ask you some questions?

DEE: Of course. Go ahead.

JANET: Does your bank require a minimum balance?

DEE: Yes. If the customer doesn't have a savings account here with a balance of at least one thousand dollars, we require a minimum balance of two hundred dollars in the checking account.

JANET: What happens if I fall below the two-hundred-dollar minimum?

DEE: There is a fifteen-dollar monthly service charge and a twenty-cent charge for each check that you write in that month.

JANET: I see. And if I keep the two-hundred-dollar balance, is there any monthly charge?

DEE: There's no charge.

JANET: Okay. I'd like to open a checking account here.

DEE: Would you rather have an individual or a joint account?

JANET: I'd rather have an individual account, thank you.

DEE: Fine, and what is the name?

JANET: Janet Parker. P-A-R-K-E-R.

DEE: All right, Ms. Parker. You'd better fill out this signature card. We need some personal information.

Janet fills out the signature card and gives it to Dee.

DEE: How much money would you like to deposit into your account?

JANET: Well, I have my paycheck here, but I don't want to deposit all of it. I'd rather deposit some of it and get a little cash back.

DEE: No problem. Just fill out the deposit slip with the amount of cash you want back, and sign your name on the line.

JANET: I'd better get about three hundred dollars in cash. I'm planning on going clothes shopping for some relaxation.

DEE: How nice. We have many different check designs. You'd better pick the checks you like. Your name, address, and telephone number will be printed on the checks. The checks are personalized.

JANET: Do you have any pink checks? I like pink.

DEE: Of course we have pink. Every month you'll receive a monthly statement showing you the checks you wrote and the deposits you made.

JANET: Yes, I know. Isn't it wonderful being independent?

Exercises

A. Answer the questions in complete sentences.

1. Why did Janet feel proud of herself?

2. What did Janet expect Ted to do?

3. What did Ted want to do for relaxation?

4. Where did Janet drop the laundry basket?

5. What does this independent woman need?

6. What minimum balance did the bank require?

7. What kind of checking account did Janet want to open?

8. What did Janet have to fill out?

9. How much cash did Janet want back?

10. What information will the bank print on Janet's personalized checks?

B. **Expression of purpose**   Complete each sentence with either **to** or **for**. Follow the examples:

> She went to the store __for__ some groceries.
> She went to the store __to__ buy some groceries.

1. He wanted to go golfing _____ some relaxation.

2. He wanted to go golfing _____ relax.

3. She was gathering dirty clothes _____ the laundry.

4. She was getting dirty clothes together _____ do the laundry.

5. Janet went to the bank _____ get her very own checking account.

6. Janet went to the bank _____ her very own checking account.

7. Dee gave Janet the signature card _____ fill out.

8. Janet wanted some cash _____ go shopping.

C.   Matching   Find the word or phrase in column B that has the same meaning as the word or phrase in column A. Write the letter of the correct answer on the line.

A	**B**
_____ 1. duties	a. should
_____ 2. gather	b. put money in the bank
_____ 3. get angry	c. get together
_____ 4. would rather	d. the least, the smallest amount
_____ 5. had better	e. prefer
_____ 6. pitch in	f. fly off the handle
_____ 7. personalized	g. chores
_____ 8. quite	h. contribute
_____ 9. minimum	i. really, very
_____ 10. deposit	j. printed with one's name

D. Would rather/had better   Practice these exchanges with a partner. Use **would rather** in the question and **had better** in the answer. Follow the example:

> **A:** <u>Would</u> you <u>rather have</u> a joint or an individual account? (have)
>
> **B:** I <u>had better get</u> an individual account. (get)

1. **A:** _____ you _____ a checking or a savings account? (open)

   B: I _____ a checking account. (open)

2. **A:** _____ Janet _____ her maiden name or her married name? (use)

   B: She _____ her married name. (use)

3. **A:** _____ you _____ golfing or do the laundry? (go)

   B: I _____ the laundry. (do)

4. **A:** _____ you and your husband _____ pink or brown checks? (have)

   B: I'd rather have pink, but I think we _____ brown ones. (order)

5. **A:** _____ you _____ cash or by check? (pay)

   B: I _____ by check. (pay)

6. **A:** _____ the Parkers _____ out or clean house? (go)

   B: They'd rather go out, but they _____ house. (clean)

7. **A:** _____ Dee Johnson _____ late or go home early?
   (work)

   B: She'd rather go home early, but she _____ late. (work)

8. **A:** _____ you _____ studying or leave for home now?
   (continue)

   B: I'd rather leave for home now, but I _____ studying.
   (continue)

E. Signature card   Read the signature card. Then answer the questions in complete sentences.

First Rancho Bank of the United States

SIGNATURE CARD

Quimby	**Rhonda**	**Lee**	**Babcock**
Last	First	Middle	Maiden

1998 Old Glory Rd.	Center City,	CA	90087
Address	City	State	Zip

555-0256	555-4329	009-44-6666
Bus. Phone	Home phone	Social Security No.

PLEASE CHECK ONE		PLEASE CHECK ONE	
Checking acct.	☒	Individual acct.	☒
Savings acct.	☐	Joint acct.	☐

Polanski

Mother's maiden name

Rhonda Quimby   September 23, 19 —

Signature	Date

1. Does she want her own account or an account with another person?

2. How do you know that she is or was married?

3. What's her social security number?

4. Is she opening a checking or a savings account?

5. What's her mother's maiden name?

6. Why do you think a bank asks for the mother's maiden name?

7. When did she open this account?

8. Does she work? How do you know?

F. **Conversation** Practice asking and answering questions with a partner. You are a bank employee. Read these instructions and ask the correct questions. Your partner must answer in complete sentences. Then, have your partner ask you the questions.

1. Ask if he or she wants a checking or a savings account.

2. Ask if he or she wants an individual or a joint account.

3. Ask what his or her social security number is.

4. Ask how he or she spells his or her last name.

5. Ask what his or her address is.

6. Ask how much he or she wants to deposit.

7. Ask if he or she already has a savings account with a bank.

8. Ask what his or her occupation is.

CHAPTER 9

Twenty Dollars Is Just Right

Vocabulary

agree (v)   think the same as someone else

following (adj)   next

furious (adj)   mad, very angry

glued (adj)   stuck, attached to

handy (adj)   clever with one's hands, able to repair things

leaky (adj)   dripping

replace (v)   put back

swear (v)   take an oath, promise

Idioms

It **drove** Janet **up the wall**.   made someone feel crazy

I guess I'll be able to **figure** it **out**.   discover an answer, calculate

It's been going on **for ages**.   for a long time

I promise—as soon as this game **is over**.   is finished, is ended

Twenty Dollars Is Just Right

Cold water has been dripping from the Parkers' bathroom faucet for several weeks. Ted told his wife not to call a plumber because a plumber would be too expensive. Their rental agreement says they must pay for small plumbing problems themselves. Ted promised to fix the faucet three weeks ago, but he hasn't done it yet.

The leaky faucet has been making Janet quite angry. She reminded her husband of his promise, and he swore that he'd fix it the following Sunday.

"That's what you told me last Sunday and the Sunday before that," Janet answered. "You swore you'd fix it, but you didn't, and it keeps on dripping. It's been going on for ages, and it's driving me crazy! I'm not kidding, Ted. If you don't fix it this weekend, I'm going to be furious. I don't want you glued to that TV again next Sunday."

Janet didn't get furious very often, but this time was different. The problem was that every Sunday morning Ted turned on a football game, and when Janet asked him to repair the faucet he said, "Okay, honey. I promise—as soon as this game is over."

However, when the first football game was over, there was another he wanted to watch. After the second game, there was a third, then a fourth, and the faucet never got fixed. Ted was stuck to the television all day long. It drove Janet up the wall.

The following Sunday was no different. Janet wouldn't speak to Ted. She worked around the house, did the laundry, and cooked dinner, but she wouldn't speak to Ted.

The next week, on her day off, Janet decided to fix the dripping bathroom faucet herself. "It can't be that difficult to repair," she thought. "I'll get Ted's toolbox out of the garage and see what I can do. I'm sure I'll be able to figure it out."

First, she looked inside the cabinet under the sink to find the water valves. Then, she turned off the cold water by closing the cold-water valve. Next, she used a screwdriver to take out the screw of the cold-water handle.

Next, she removed a nut and a washer. Then, she took out the stem. She found an old washer under the stem. It was completely worn-out.

"That's it!" Janet shouted. "This old washer has been causing the leak. All I need to do is replace it with a new one."

Janet looked inside her husband's toolbox to find another washer of the same size. Luckily, she found one.

Janet put the new washer in place and then replaced all of the faucet parts: the stem, the nut, the other washer, the handle, and the screw. Finally, she opened the cold-water valve and turned on the water to check for leaking. Everything worked perfectly. There was no leak.

"Well, that was easy enough," Janet said to herself, "and to think I waited for almost a month for my lazy husband to stop watching football and fix it!"

It is Wednesday evening. Ted is in the bathroom brushing his teeth. Ted sees that the faucet is not leaking anymore.

TED: Hey, Janet! Look at this! The faucet stopped dripping all by itself. Isn't that great? I won't have to fix it after all.

JANET: Oh, Ted! It didn't stop by itself. Someone took care of it.

TED: Janet, did you call a plumber? That's so expensive. I told you that I was going to do it.

JANET: Relax, hon. I didn't call a plumber.

TED: You didn't? Then who . . . ? How . . . ? What happened?

JANET: Someone who lives in our neighborhood did it.

TED: Really? That's great. Who was it? That old guy next
       door?

JANET: No, not him. It was somebody very handy. A
         handyperson. Someone who can figure things out.

TED: That's great! Maybe we should pay this handyperson.
       What do you think, Janet? How about twenty dollars?

JANET: Oh, I agree with you, Ted. I think this handyperson
         should get paid, and I think twenty dollars is just right.

Exercises

A.   Answer the questions in complete sentences.

1. Why did Ted tell Janet not to call a plumber?

2. What's been driving Janet crazy?

3. What was Ted stuck to all Sunday long?

4. What did Janet decide to do on her day off?

5. How did Janet turn off the cold water?

6. What did she find under the stem?

7. What did she find in Ted's toolbox?

8. What did Janet receive for her services?

B.   Matching   Find the word or phrase in column B that has the same meaning as the word or phrase in column A. Write the letter of the correct answer on the line.

A	B
_____ 1. mad	a. put back
_____ 2. promised	b. discover
_____ 3. dripping	c. for a long time
_____ 4. glued	d. finished
_____ 5. over	e. next
_____ 6. for ages	f. swore
_____ 7. make someone crazy	g. furious
_____ 8. figure out	h. stuck
_____ 9. replace	i. leaky
_____ 10. following	j. drive someone up the wall

C.   Say/tell   Complete each sentence with either **said** or **told**.

1. She _____ him to take care of it.

2. He _____ he would fix it.

3. Ted _____ a plumber could be expensive.

4. Mrs. Parker _____ the plumber to come right away.

5. Mr. Parker _____ his wife to wait.

6. They _____ that the faucet was dripping.

7. He _____ her to turn off the hot water.

8. We _____ them to get the wrench and the screwdriver.

9. You _____ that dinner would be ready soon.

10. I _____ you to repair it yourself.

D. Present perfect Complete each sentence with the negative form of the present perfect tense. Follow the example:

> He promised to fix it a week ago, but he
> <u>hasn't repaired</u> it yet. (repair)

1. She said she would call a plumber, but she _____ one yet. (call)

2. He swore that he would do it, but he _____ it yet. (do)

3. They tried to leave early, but they _____ yet. (leave)

4. Her husband planned on fixing it, but he _____ care of it yet. (take)

5. They've been married for two years, but they _____ a baby yet. (have)

6. She's been up since 6:00 A.M. but she _____ breakfast yet. (eat)

7. Mr. Parker has worked there for a long time, but the company _____ him a vacation yet. (give)

8. The plumber charged them fifty dollars, but they
_____ him yet. (pay)

9. She's been in the hardware store for fifteen minutes, but a
salesperson _____ her yet. (help)

10. I thought they were coming at 8:00 P.M., but they
_____ yet. (arrive)

E. Present perfect continuous Change each present perfect
sentence to the present perfect continuous. Follow the example:

It's dripped for a long time.

It's been dripping for a long time.

1. It's driven her up the wall for a long time.

2. It's leaked for ages.

3. She's asked him to fix it for three weeks.

4. He's promised to fix it since last week.

5. That plumber has repaired faucets for many years.

6. She's spoken to him about the leak.

7. He's watched TV since early this morning.

8. They've lived in that house for ages.

9. They've talked about moving.

10. We've worked in the kitchen all morning.

F. Be/do   Practice the dialogue with a partner. Use **was, wasn't, were, weren't, did,** or **didn't.**

A: Janet _____ upset about the leaky faucet.

B: I know she _____ . _____ she call a plumber?

A: No, she _____ . Ted _____ going to fix it.

B: What happened? _____ he fix the leak?

A: No, he _____ . He _____ promising to do it, but he always had one more game to watch.

B: _____ they argue about it? _____ they mad at each other?

A: Yes, they _____ . But they _____ angry for very long. Janet took care of everything. She replaced an old washer and got twenty dollars for it.

B: How in the world _____ she get twenty dollars?

A: It _____ hard because Ted _____ so happy to pay the handyperson for fixing that dripping faucet. He _____ know it was Janet.

G. Five steps Explain how to do something in five or more steps. Follow the example:

QUESTION: How do you use a washing machine?

ANSWER: First, I put my clothes in the machine.
Then I choose my temperature and cycle settings.
Next, I start the machine.
Then I add my soap.
Finally, I close the lid and wait.

1. How do you use a public telephone?

2. How do you write and mail a letter?

3. How do you fix a flat tire?

4. How do you make coffee?

5. How do you wash the dishes?

6. How do you use a parking meter?

7. How do you use a cassette tape player?

8. How do you change a baby's diaper?

9. How do you use a candy machine?

10. How do you sew on a button?

11. How do you wrap a birthday present?

12. How do you take the bus?

13. How do you eat an apple?

14. How do you sharpen your pencil?

15. How do you repair a leaky faucet?

CHAPTER 10

Make It Light

Vocabulary

attractive (adj) good-looking

beer belly (n) a large stomach on a person who drinks too much beer

ingredients (n) foods and mixtures used to make a food product

load (v) fill

loaded (adj) full

overeat (v) eat too much

produce (n) fresh fruits and vegetables

protein (foods) (n) foods like eggs, meat, fish, and milk

sodium (n) salt (sodium chloride)

Idioms

Janet had **put on a few pounds**. gained weight

I've **eaten like a pig** for months. overeaten

I haven't **paid attention** to my diet. observed, watched

He didn't think she was fat **at all**. not in the least

Now I'm **paying the price**. suffering the consequences of one's past actions

It's time for me to **go on a diet**. eat a certain amount of food so as to lose weight

Make It Light

Ted was in the kitchen fixing breakfast. He called to Janet who was in the bedroom getting dressed.

"Hey, Janet," he shouted, "do you want bacon with your eggs?"

"No! No bacon!" she shouted back. Janet was having trouble zipping up her jeans. She was trying to take a deep breath and hold in her stomach so she could zip them up. It was a little difficult. Janet had put on a few pounds.

"I've gotten chubby, Ted," she said as she walked into the kitchen. "I've eaten like a pig for months, and now I'm fat. I've been overeating every day since your boss's birthday dinner. I haven't paid attention to my diet, and I've put on too many pounds. It's time for me to go on a diet. No bacon for me, Ted. And no toast with jam. I'll have an egg and some juice. That's all."

Ted was a little surprised by Janet's decision. He didn't think she was fat at all.

"I think you look sexy, Janet," he told her. "I like you this way."

"Sexy! How can you say I look sexy when I'm fat!" she said.

Ted tried to tell her that she wasn't overweight. He tried to tell her that she looked healthy and attractive, but Janet wouldn't listen to him at all.

"I looked attractive a couple of months ago," she said, "but since that birthday dinner for your boss, I've done nothing but eat, eat, eat, and now I'm paying the price. You should go on a diet, too, Ted. You're looking a little chubby yourself."

Ted and Janet agreed that they hadn't been watching their diets very carefully. They agreed that they needed to plan healthier meals.

Ted and Janet are grocery shopping. Janet is carefully reading the ingredients on the food labels. Ted is following her, pushing the cart. Janet shows Ted the ingredients of the breakfast cereal they usually buy.

JANET: Look at this, Ted. The first ingredient listed on the box is sugar. Do you know what that means? It means that this cereal is mostly sugar.

TED: Mostly sugar? I didn't know that. We've bought this cereal for years. Well, let's try one of these natural grain cereals. Here's one. The box says no sugar added.

JANET: That's fine. How about some tuna? I'll make tuna salad.

TED: That sounds good. Tuna is good protein. Let's get the tuna packed in water, not the tuna packed in oil.

JANET: Of course. I haven't bought tuna in oil since last year. I stopped that a long time ago.

TED: Oh, I didn't know that. How about some big, juicy steaks?

JANET: Maybe we should eat more chicken and fish, Ted. For many years, doctors have said that Americans eat too much red meat.

TED: Really? I didn't know that. But you're right. We just had steaks a couple of days ago. And hamburgers last night. Hey, look! Peanuts! Let's get some.

JANET: Oh, Ted, those peanuts are loaded with sodium. Too much salt isn't good for your blood pressure.

TED: But we haven't had peanuts in the house since last Christmas. Here. We can get the unsalted ones. See? No salt.

JANET: Okay, but let's go over to the produce section. We need to load our cart with fresh fruits and vegetables.

TED: You go ahead. I'll meet you there. I'm going to get a six-pack of beer.

JANET: Make it light beer.

TED: Light? Why?

JANET: Are you kidding? With your beer belly?

Exercises

A.   Answer the questions in complete sentences.

1. What was Ted doing in the kitchen?

2. Since when has Janet been overeating?

3. What did Ted think about Janet's weight?

4. Why didn't Ted and Janet buy their usual cereal?

5. How did Janet know that the cereal was mostly sugar?

6. Why do you think Janet stopped buying tuna in oil?

7. What have doctors said about Americans for many years?

8. With what did Janet want to load their cart?

B. True or false   Read each sentence. Write **T** on the line if the sentence is true. Write **F** on the line if it is false.

_____ 1. Doctors tell Americans that they eat too much red meat.

_____ 2. Janet says that she has been eating too much and that now she must pay the price. This means that Janet is going to pay for the groceries.

_____ 3. Eggs, meat, fish, and milk are examples of protein foods.

_____ 4. Sodium is salt.

_____ 5. Fresh fruits and vegetables are found in the dairy section of the supermarket.

_____ 6. Too much salt in your diet can be bad for your blood pressure.

C. Present perfect/past   Complete each sentence with the correct present perfect or past form of the verb. Follow the examples:

> Ted ____bought____ light beer yesterday. (buy)
> Ted __has bought__ light beer for a long time. (buy)

1. Janet _____ since the boss's birthday dinner. (overeat)

2. The Parkers _____ attention to their diets for months. (not/pay)

3. Ted _____ peanuts since last Christmas. (not/buy)

4. For many years, doctors _____ Americans to eat less red meat. (tell)

5. They _____ a long time ago that too much sodium could be bad for their blood pressure. (learn)

6. Since his heart attack, Ted's boss _____ on a low-sodium diet. (be)

7. Americans _____ too much red meat for too many years. (eat)

8. I _____ a cup of coffee since last month. (not/have)

D. Past/present perfect negative with *for* or *since* Practice asking and answering questions with a partner. Ask the questions in the past tense. Answer the questions in the present perfect negative using **for** or **since**. Follow the example:

A: When __did__ she __begin__ to buy tuna in water? (begin)

B: Oh, she __hasn't bought__ tuna in oil __for__ a year. (not/buy)

1. A: When _____ his boss _____ smoking? (quit)

   B: Oh, his boss _____ a cigarette _____ 1984. (not/smoke)

2. A: Why _____ she _____ chicken and fish but no red meat? (buy)

   B: She _____ red meat _____ she saw her doctor. (not/buy)

3. **A:** When _____ Ted _____ to drink light beer? (start)

   B: Oh, he _____ regular beer _____ his wife told him to buy light. (not/have)

4. **A:** Why _____ they _____ unsalted peanuts? (get)

   B: Oh, they _____ salted peanuts _____ they learned about sodium. (not/get)

5. **A:** When _____ Janet _____ to put on so many pounds? (begin)

   B: She _____ attention to her diet _____ about three months. (not/pay)

6. **A:** Why _____ you _____ your cart with fresh fruits? (load)

   B: Oh, I _____ canned fruits _____ years. (not/get)

7. **A:** When _____ the Parkers _____ buying that cereal? (stop)

   B: Oh, they _____ that cereal _____ they learned that it was loaded with sugar. (not/like)

8. **A:** Why _____ you _____ nothing but fresh produce? (choose)

   B: I _____ any kind of meat _____ many, many years. (not/eat) I'm a vegetarian.

E.   Read the following labels and answer the questions in complete sentences.

CORN FLAKES CEREAL

Ingredients: corn, sugar, corn syrup, molasses, salt, vegetable oil, artificial color.

CHICKEN SOUP

Ingredients: chicken stock, egg noodles, chicken, water, salt, monosodium glutamate, garlic.

BIG CATCH TUNA

Servings 2

NUTRITION INFORMATION PER SERVING

Protein ....12 gm
Carbohydrates .... 0 gm
Fat .... 2 gm
Sodium ....310 mg

Ingredients: tuna, water, salt.

Packed in water.

---

1. Does the chicken soup have more noodles or chicken? How do you know?

2. The chicken soup contains salt and monosodium glutamate (MSG). What do you think MSG is?

3. How many kinds of sugar can you find in the breakfast cereal? Name them.

4. Why do you think that this breakfast cereal is not the best cereal for children?

5. How many servings of tuna are in the can?

6. How much protein is in one serving? How much sodium?

7. Why do you think that this tuna is bad for someone with high blood pressure?

8. Tell about some foods that you can't eat, and explain why.

F. **Conversation**   How about you?

1. Have you put on a couple of pounds recently? Why or why not?

2. Tell about a time when you overate.

3. Do you usually read the labels on the products you buy? Why or why not?

4. How often do you eat fish?

5. What sugar-free or salt-free products do you buy?

6. Talk about grocery shopping in your native country.

CHAPTER 11

About Four Loads

Vocabulary

chlorine bleach (n)   a liquid that makes clothes white

bore (n)   a dull or boring time

fade (v)   lose color

gentle (adj)   delicate, soft

load (n)   quantity of clothes in the washer or dryer

permanent press (adj)   nonwrinkling (no ironing needed)

pile (v)   stack, put one on top of the other

shrink (v)   get smaller

tumble dry (v)   dry clothes in the dryer

wring (v)   twist

Idioms

He has **taken on** more **responsibilities.**   become responsible for more things

I**'m** not **used to** doing household chores.   accustomed to

Maybe we should **let the house go** this Saturday.   forget about cleaning the house

He wasn't **looking forward to** doing housework.   anticipating, looking happily to a future event

We'll **get it out of the way.**   finish something so as to have free time

About Four Loads

Since the time that Janet got mad at Ted for not sharing the housework, he has taken on more responsibilities around the house. He realized that Janet had reason to be angry. He knew it wasn't right to expect her to take care of the housework on top of her job. Ted really didn't want to vacuum or wash dishes or clean bathrooms, but neither did Janet. He wasn't having any fun doing housework, but Janet wasn't either.

"You know, Janet," he said one evening while he was drying dishes as she washed, "I'm not used to doing household chores after working hard all day."

"Neither am I," Janet responded.

"Saturday mornings are really a bore these days. Do you realize that I haven't gone golfing on a Saturday morning for weeks? I haven't had any Saturday relaxation in a long time."

"I haven't either, Ted," Janet said.

"Maybe we should let the house go this Saturday, just forget it completely. I'll make a golf date, and you can go shopping. Buy yourself another pair of shoes or something."

Ted wasn't looking forward to starting another weekend with housework. Neither was Janet, he hoped.

To his surprise, Janet told him that she thought letting the house go was a great idea.

"You're absolutely right, Ted," she told him. "You're not married to this house, and I'm not either. We can let it go for one weekend. It won't kill us. But we'll need clean clothes for next week, so I don't think we should forget about the laundry."

"Neither do I," Ted agreed. "Let's do the laundry Friday evening. We'll get it out of the way and have the weekend free."

It is Friday evening. Ted and Janet are doing the laundry together. Janet has always done the laundry. Ted is inexperienced.

TED: Wow! We have a lot of laundry here, but I think we can probably wash everything in two big loads.

JANET: Two loads? What are you talking about? We'll have to make about four loads.

TED: Why four? That'll take twice the time. There's a ball game I want to watch on TV. Just throw everything in hot water and get it out of the way.

JANET: Oh, Ted, we can't do that. If we wash my cotton blouses in hot water, they'll shrink and fade.

TED: Okay. You take care of your clothes, and I'll take care of mine. Let me use the washer first. I'm going to wash all of my sweaters and shirts and pants.

JANET: You'd better not wash your sweaters in the machine. Read the labels. They say **Hand wash cold. Do not twist or wring. Dry flat.**

TED: Holy cow, Janet. This is going to take all night. I want to watch that ball game. Why don't we take everything to the dry cleaner's?

JANET: Are you kidding? That would cost an arm and a leg! Look, it's easy. Wash cottons in cold water, permanent press in warm, sheets and towels in hot. Don't use chlorine bleach on any of the colors, only on whites. Put things in the dryer only when the label says **Tumble dry.** If you remember these things, Ted, laundry will be easy for you.

TED: If you take care of it all, it'll really be easy for me! I want to watch that game.

JANET: All right. I'll help you separate your clothes into different piles. Then you can wash your own clothes when you want to.

TED: Great! Tell me what to do.

JANET: Read all the labels. Labels tell you how to care for clothes. Put all the cottons in one pile. Put all the polyester and permanent press in another pile, and wash them on the gentle cycle. Make a small pile for hand washables. I'll take care of the sheets and towels.

TED: Janet, you're the greatest. I love you. I'll wash my clothes Sunday evening, right after the tennis match.

Exercises

A.   Answer the questions in complete sentences.

1. What has Ted done since the time that Janet got mad at him?

2. What is Ted not used to doing?

3. What did Janet think was a great idea?

4. What will they need for next week?

5. How many loads of laundry will they have to make?

6. If they wash Janet's cotton blouses in hot water, what will happen?

7. What do the labels on Ted's sweaters say?

8. When can you put things in the dryer?

9. What do labels tell you?

10. Who'll take care of the sheets and towels?

B. Matching Find the each word or phrase in column B that has the same meaning as the word or phrase in column A. Write the letter of the correct answer on the line.

A	**B**
_____ 1. tumble dry	a. anticipate
_____ 2. permanent press	b. a boring time
_____ 3. gentle cycle	c. get smaller
_____ 4. do not wring	d. stack of laundry
_____ 5. shrink	e. dry in the dryer
_____ 6. fade	f. do not twist
_____ 7. a load	g. quantity of clothes in the washer
_____ 8. pile of clothes	h. delicate cycle
_____ 9. a bore	i. no ironing needed
_____ 10. look forward to	j. lose color.

C. *Either* in negative sentences Complete each sentence with the correct negative helping verb. Follow the example:

> Ted doesn't like to do laundry, and
> Janet <u>doesn't</u> either.

1. Ted didn't want to vacuum the carpets, and Janet _____ either.

2. Ted isn't used to doing household chores after working all day, and Janet _____ either.

3. He wasn't having any fun, and she _____ either.

4. He hasn't gone golfing in a long time, and his friends _____ either.

5. They weren't looking forward to more housework, and he _____ either.

6. I don't like to do laundry, and my husband _____ either.

7. The colors shouldn't be washed in hot water, and the cottons _____ either.

8. We haven't cleaned the house in more than a week, and our neighbor _____ either.

9. Ted doesn't want to wash his sweaters by hand, and I _____ either.

10. The refrigerator wasn't working well, and the washer and dryer _____ either.

D. *Neither* **in negative sentences**   Complete each sentence with the correct affirmative helping verb. Follow the example:

> Ted doesn't like to do laundry, and neither
> _____does_____ Janet.

1. Cottons can't be washed in hot water, and neither _____ these sweaters.

2. Bleach isn't good for permanent press clothing, and neither _____ hot water.

3. I haven't had any relaxation for a long time, and neither _____ Ted.

4. Janet didn't look forward to housework, and neither _____ Ted.

5. He wasn't taking on more responsibility, and neither _____ his brothers.

6. Ted and Janet don't enjoy working Saturday mornings, and neither _____ I.

7. Hot water shouldn't hurt these white sheets, and neither _____ bleach.

8. I haven't separated the clothes, and neither _____ Janet.

9. Ted won't do the laundry until Sunday, and neither _____ I.

10. We don't want the weekends to be a bore, and neither _____ Ted.

E. Conditionals Practice these exchanges with a partner.
Follow the example:

> **A:** What will happen if I wash the cotton clothes in
> hot water?
>
> **B:** If you wash the cotton clothes in hot water, they
> ___will shrink___ . (shrink)

1. **A:** What will happen if Ted puts his red shirt in hot water?

   B: If he puts his red shirt in hot water, it _____ . (fade)

2. **A:** What will happen if they can't agree?

   B: If they can't agree, they _____ mad. (get)

3. **A:** What will happen if he tumble dries his sweater?

   B: If he tumble dries his sweater, it _____ . (shrink)

4. **A:** What will happen if Ted watches the ball game?

   B: If Ted _____ the ball game, he _____ his laundry.
   (watch) (not/do)

5. **A:** What will happen if they don't separate the clothes?

   B: If they _____ the clothes, the colors _____ . (not/
   separate) (fade)

6. **A:** What'll happen if Janet goes shopping on Saturday?

    B: If Janet _____ shopping on Saturday, she _____ probably _____ another pair of shoes. (go) (buy)

7. **A:** What'll happen if they let the house go?

    B: If they _____ the house go, it _____ dirtier. (let) (get)

8. **A:** What'll happen if Janet doesn't work full-time?

    B: If Janet _____ full-time they _____ able to make ends meet. (not/work) (not/be)

9. **A:** What'll happen if Janet's mother comes to visit?

    B: If Janet's mother _____ to visit, she _____ to sleep on the new sofa. (come) (have)

10. **A:** What'll happen if they don't put the clothes in piles?

    B: If they _____ the clothes in piles, the permanent press _____ mixed up with the cottons. (not/put) (get)

F. Clothing labels Look at the labels. Then read the sentences. Write the letter of the correct answer on the line.

a.

50% COTTON 50% POLYESTER
Machine wash cold
Tumble dry
Remove promptly

b.

100% WOOL
Dry clean only

c.

Hand wash separately
Line dry
Do not twist
Press with cool iron

d.

100% RAYON
Machine wash warm
Gentle cycle
Do not bleach

_____ 1. This garment can't be washed.

_____ 2. Hang it on a hanger to dry.

_____ 3. Put your washer on delicate for this garment.

_____ 4. You can put this article of clothing in the dryer.

_____ 5. If you wring this garment, it'll probably lose its shape.

_____ 6. This article of clothing is made of sheep hair.

_____ 7. It may fade, so don't wash it with your other clothes.

_____ 8. Take it out of the dryer while it's still warm.

_____ 9. Bleaching this garment will probably make it fade.

_____ 10. Don't use a hot iron.

G. Conversation   How about you?

1. How often do you do your laundry? Why?

2. Do you often go to a laundromat?

3. What pieces of clothing do you own that you can't wash in hot water? Why not?

4. Have any of your clothes ever shrunk or faded? Tell about it.

5. Do you prefer to buy clothes made of cotton, polyester, nylon, or _____ ? Why?

6. How often do you iron? What do you do while you're ironing?

7. Do you always use a dryer, or do you sometimes line dry your clothes? Why?

8. Do you own more clothes for hot weather or for cold weather? Which kind of clothes are easier to care for? Why?

CHAPTER 12

Don't Touch Anything

Vocabulary

belongings (n)   possessions, things that belong to a person

burglarize (v)   rob a home

dead bolt (n)   a safe door lock that throws a metal bolt into the side of the doorway

engrave (v)   write numbers (or names) into metal, wood, or plastic

neighborhood watch (n)   a program in which neighbors work together to prevent crime

organize (v)   make a plan, gather people for action

suspicious (adj)   looking as if something is wrong

VCR (n)   video cassette recorder

Idioms

They didn't **make a habit of** going out.   do something routinely

They wanted to go out for dinner **once in a while**.   sometimes, now and then, occasionally

They discovered how the burglar had **broken in**.   entered a place illegally

Every neighbor **takes part in** watching for something suspicious.   participates

Don't Touch Anything

Although Ted and Janet didn't make a habit of going out anymore, last Friday they met for dinner after work. They didn't think that going out for dinner once in a while would hurt their budget.

They chose to meet at a little Italian restaurant that had fantastic dinner specials. "You can't find a better bargain anywhere," Ted insisted. "This is the most reasonable restaurant in town."

Ted and Janet enjoyed the meal, but they planned to spend the rest of the evening economically. They planned to go home and watch an old, romantic movie on television. Janet wanted to record it on their VCR.

When they got home, however, Ted and Janet discovered that their evening plans were impossible. Someone had robbed them.

"Holy cow, Janet! Look at this place! It's a mess. We've been burglarized!" Ted was shocked, and so was Janet.

"How could this have happened?" Janet asked. "We always lock our doors."

It didn't take them very long to discover how the burglar had broken in. The lock on the kitchen door was broken. The kitchen door was open.

Ted and Janet found out that their stereo was gone. Their TV and VCR were too. The bedroom was a mess, and so was the closet.

"Honey," Janet called. "All of my jewelry's been stolen. And so have your golf clubs!"

"What?" Ted couldn't believe it. "The burglar took my golf clubs? Well, that does it, Janet! That does it! Let's call the police."

Ted called the police department. Since it wasn't an emergency, he didn't dial 911. "Don't clean and don't touch anything," the dispatcher said. "The police will want to check for fingerprints."

Within the hour, two officers arrive at Ted and Janet's house.

JENKINS: Hello. I'm Officer Jenkins. This is my partner, Officer Swanson. We're here in answer to your call. Can you tell us exactly what happened?

TED: Well, my wife and I went out to dinner after work, and when we came home we found that our house had been burglarized. Whoever it was broke the kitchen door lock.

SWANSON: Did you see anyone inside or leaving your home?

TED: No, we didn't.

JENKINS: I know that you haven't had much time to investigate, but can you tell us what is missing?

JANET: All of my jewelry is gone. Everything! Even the cheap stuff. And Ted's golf clubs. And, of course, our TV, stereo, and VCR.

JENKINS: Were any of your possessions engraved with your state driver's license number?

TED: No. We didn't do that.

SWANSON: That's too bad. If you had your California driver's license number engraved on your belongings, the police department would be able to identify your things. We need positive identification to be able to return possessions. Engraving is one way.

JANET: I certainly can't engrave my driver's license number on my jewelry!

JENKINS: No, you can't. You should take photographs of your jewelry.

TED: Where can I get an engraver?

SWANSON: You can borrow one from the police department. There's no charge. Just show some identification. The engraver works on plastic, metal, or wood.

JANET: Thank you, Officer. That's good to know. What about our locks? I thought our door locks were safe, but this kitchen door lock was broken easily.

JENKINS: The best kind of lock to have is a dead bolt. The button locks in doorknobs are no good at all. If you had a dead bolt on your kitchen door, a burglar probably wouldn't be able to break in.

SWANSON: And when you go on vacation, be sure to stop delivery of your mail and newspaper. A burglar knows that no one is home when he or she sees a bunch of newspapers on the doorstep.

JANET: Oh, when we took our last vacation, we asked our neighbor to get our mail for us.

JENKINS: Also, you and your neighbors could organize a neighborhood watch. If you had a neighborhood watch, you wouldn't be easy victims of burglary.

TED: What can we do to start a neighborhood watch?

SWANSON: Talk to your neighbors first. See if they're interested. Then call the police department and make an appointment. All the neighbors get together and listen to an officer's instructions on how to become a neighborhood watch community. It's easy.

JENKINS: That's right. And every neighbor takes part in watching for anything suspicious. The neighbors work together to prevent crime.

TED: I think I'll organize a neighborhood watch before I buy a new set of golf clubs. Thank you, Officers.

Exercises

A.   Answer the questions in complete sentences.

1. Why did Ted and Janet think that going out for dinner last Friday was okay?

2. What happened when they got home?

3. What was broken?

4. Why didn't Ted dial 911?

5. What should Ted engrave on his possessions?

6. What should Janet do to her jewelry?

7. Where could Ted and Janet get an engraver?

8. What should a person do when he or she goes on vacation?

9. What's the best door lock?

10. What does every neighbor do to prevent crime?

B.   Take one out   Read each of the word groups. Take out the word or phrase that does not belong.

1. TV, VCR, jewelry, stereo

2. burglar, officer, thief, robber

3. organize, belongings, possessions, things

4. engrave, identify, driver's license number, break in

5. 911, chain lock, dead bolt, button lock

6. burglarized, prevents, stole, organized

7. break in, enter illegally, take part in

8. occasionally, once in a while, make a habit of, sometimes

C. *So* **in positive sentences** Complete each sentence with the correct helping verb. Follow the example:

Ted was shocked, and so __was__ Janet.

1. Their house was burglarized, and so _____ ours.

2. Their stereo was gone, and so _____ their TV and VCR.

3. Janet thought burglary wasn't possible, and so _____ Ted.

4. I always forget to lock the door, and so _____ she.

5. Her jewelry's been stolen, and so _____ his golf clubs.

6. The police know about the burglary, and so _____ the neighbors.

7. The police are coming, and so _____ Janet's mother.

8. Our neighbors took part in the neighborhood watch, and so _____ we.

9. A burglar could easily break this lock, and so _____ I.

10. Janet's been careless, and so _____ Ted.

D. *Too* **in positive sentences**   Complete each sentence with
the correct helping verb. Follow the example:

> Their stereo was gone, and their TV and VCR
> __were__ too.

1. The bedroom was a mess, and the closet _____ too.

2. Ted waited patiently for the police, and Janet _____ too.

3. The police want to prevent crime, and the neighbors _____
    too.

4. The windows are locked, and the door _____ too.

5. Ted and Janet have discovered a robbery, and their neighbor
    _____ too.

6. Ted's going to organize a neighborhood watch, and I _____
    too.

7. I've made a habit of locking my doors, and my sister _____
    too.

8. Our neighbor put in a dead bolt, and Ted _____ too.

9. Her jewelry was stolen, and his golf clubs _____ too.

10. She's had her mail stopped, and I _____ too.

E.   Conditionals   Practice these exchanges with a partner.
Follow the example:

> **A:** What would happen if they put in a dead bolt?
>
> **B:** If they put in a dead bolt, a burglar
>   _wouldn't break in_ . (not/break in)

1. **A:** What would happen if you engraved your driver's license
   number on your belongings?

   B: If I engraved my driver's license number on my
   belongings, the police _____ able to return my
   things to me. (be)

2. **A:** What would happen if you had a button lock in your front
   door?

   B: If I had a button lock in my front door, I _____ a
   dead bolt. (install)

3. **A:** What would they do if they came home and found their
   house burglarized?

   B: If they came home and found their house burglarized, they
   _____ the police. (call)

4. **A:** What would happen if Janet left her house unlocked?

   B: If Janet left her house unlocked, someone _____
   her possessions. (steal)

5. **A:** What would happen if you didn't have your driver's license
   number engraved on your possessions?

B: If I didn't have my driver's license number engraved on my possessions, the police _____ that the things were mine. (not/know)

6. **A:** What would you do if you lived in a neighborhood with a lot of crime?

   B: If I _____ in a neighborhood with a lot of crime, I _____ part in a neighborhood watch. (live) (take)

7. **A:** What would Ted do if he bought an expensive stereo?

   B: If Ted _____ an expensive stereo, he _____ it with his state driver's license number. (buy) (engrave)

8. **A:** What would happen if Ted and Janet had renter's insurance?

   B: If Ted and Janet _____ renter's insurance, they _____ some money for their stolen belongings. (have) (get)

9. **A:** What would Ted do if he had dead bolts on the doors?

   B: If Ted _____ dead bolts on the doors, he _____ worried about burglars. (have) (not/be)

10. **A:** What would happen if Ted and Janet organized a neighborhood watch?

    B: If Ted and Janet _____ a neighborhood watch, all the neighbors _____ safer. (organize) (feel)

F. What do you think? Read each situation and decide if what the person does is safe or not safe. Write **That's safe** or **That's not safe** on the line. If the situation is not safe, explain what needs to be done.

_____ 1. Ted installed dead bolts in both the kitchen door and the front door.

_____ 2. Ted's neighbor has left for vacation. His newspapers are piling up at his front door.

_____ 3. There's a knock at your door. You open it to see who it is.

_____ 4. Ted and Janet took photos of their valuable possessions.

_____ 5. They also engraved Ted's driver's license number on the TV, VCR, and stereo.

_____ 6. When the Parkers' neighbor got home, he saw that a window was broken and his front door was open. He immediately ran into the house.

_____ 7. It's so hot! The Parkers are going to leave their windows open while they're at work. They want some fresh air in the house.

_____ 8. Most apartment builders install only button locks.

G.   Play a game

With your class, divide into groups—group A and group B. If you
are a member of group A, write the beginning of the question
What would you do if . . . ? on a small piece of paper. If you
are a member of group B, write the beginning of the sentence **I
would . . .** on a small piece of paper. Then finish the question or
sentence. As you work, do not discuss your question or sentence
with other students. When you are finished, fold your piece of
paper in half.

   One student collects all the questions, and another student
collects all the sentences. The student who collected the
questions selects one and reads it to the class. The student who
collected the sentences selects one and reads it as an answer to
the question. The two students repeat this until they have read all
the questions and answers.

   Do the answers to the questions make sense? Are they funny,
or strange? Try this game again with different questions and
answers.

CHAPTER 13

I Could Have Screamed

Vocabulary

awfully (adv)   terribly

claim (v)   ask for, demand

confirm (v)   verify, say that a story is true

dependable (adj)   reliable, responsible

fluid (n)   liquid

properly (adv)   correctly

recommend (v)   refer, tell someone about good service

sue (v)   take legal action against

witness (n)   a person who testifies in court

Idioms

He'll have to **show up** in court.   appear or arrive at a place

Janet **found out** that the clutch was still leaking.   discovered, learned

Make up your mind.   decide

Janet **dropped** her car **off**.   left someone or something at a place

I'm tired of getting **stepped on**.   treated unfairly

He **had the nerve** to tell me there was nothing wrong.   acted boldly or impolitely

I Could Have Screamed

Janet has decided to sue an auto mechanic. She's going to take him to small-claims court. Janet won't need a lawyer because there are no attorneys in small-claims court. The money she'll be claiming from the mechanic is under two thousand dollars, so she can go to court and tell her story to the judge without a lawyer. Janet is going to sue the mechanic for $375 plus court fees.

This is how it happened. A little while ago, Janet needed to have her clutch fixed. It was leaking fluid, and it was quite difficult for her to shift gears. Janet's neighbor recommended a mechanic who was supposed to be very reliable. Because of this recommendation, Janet made an appointment and dropped her car off early Monday morning.

"Good morning," Janet said to the mechanic. "My name is Parker. I have an appointment to get my clutch fixed. It's awfully hard for me to shift gears, and an oily liquid is leaking from under the pedal."

"No problem. I fix standard transmissions all the time. I'll take care of this for you right away," the mechanic told her. "You can pick your car up around four o'clock."

Janet returned later that afternoon and paid the mechanic by check. Because she believed that he was dependable, she didn't ask any questions. Later that same week, however, Janet found out that the clutch was still leaking. She found the same oily fluid under the pedal. Once again it was hard for her to shift gears.

When she returned to the mechanic, he wouldn't listen to her. He said that he had fixed the clutch properly and told her that he couldn't help her. When Janet got home that evening, she was awfully upset.

TED: Hi, Janet. How did it go with the mechanic? Did he do things correctly this time?

JANET: Oh! That man was impossible!

TED: What do you mean? What happened?

JANET: I took the car back and explained that the clutch was giving me the same problems.

TED: Did you show him the oily fluid coming from the clutch pedal?

JANET: Yes, I did. He had the nerve to tell me that there was nothing wrong. I could have screamed.

TED: Take it easy, honey. Did you tell him that it was still hard to shift?

JANET: Yes, I did. He had the nerve to tell me that a woman shouldn't drive a stick shift. I could have choked him!

TED: Calm down, honey. Did you tell him that you wanted him to fix it or give you your money back?

JANET: Yes, I did. He had the nerve to tell me that more clutch repairs would cost me another three hundred dollars. I could have hit him with his own screwdriver!

TED: Take it easy, honey. How about if I go with you tomorrow? I'll explain things to him. Maybe if a man talks to him, he'll listen.

JANET: No, Ted. Not this time. I've made up my mind. I'm going to take care of this myself. I'm tired of getting stepped on by dishonest people. I've decided to sue him. I'm going to take that awful mechanic to small-claims court.

TED: But, Janet, a lawyer costs a lot of money.

JANET: There are no attorneys in small-claims court. It's very simple. I'll go to the court clerk at the courthouse, complete the papers, and pay a small fee. I'll write down how much money I want from the mechanic, including court fees. The marshal can serve the papers on the mechanic. The mechanic will have to show up in court, and I'll tell my story to the judge.

TED: Good for you, Janet. Is there anything I can do to help?

JANET: Yes, there is. I'm going to need a witness. Will you come to court with me to verify my case?

TED: Of course. I'd be proud to be your witness and confirm everything.

JANET: And will you do one more thing for me?

TED: Anything, honey.

JANET: Will you hold me? I think I'm going to cry.

Exercises

A. Answer the questions in complete sentences.

1. What has Janet decided to do?

2. Why doesn't she need a lawyer?

3. How much money is Janet claiming?

4. What was wrong with Janet's car?

5. Who recommended the mechanic?

6. What did Janet find out later that week?

7. Where does Janet have to go to fill out the court papers?

8. What will Janet write on the form?

B. **Multiple choice**   Choose **a, b,** or **c** as the correct answer.

1. A witness in court is someone who can _____ your case.

   a. understand

   b. confirm

   c. recommend

2. A neighbor recommended the mechanic. This means that a neighbor _____ .

   a. said the mechanic was very good

   b. said the mechanic was expensive

   c. said the mechanic had time to fix the clutch

3. The mechanic has to show up in court. This means that he must _____ .

   a. phone the judge before going to court

   b. bring a witness to court

   c. go to court on the court date

4. Janet found out that the clutch was leaking. This means that she _____ .

   a. told the mechanic that the clutch was leaking

   b. discovered that the clutch was leaking

   c. was upset that the clutch was leaking

5. Janet said, "I've made up my mind." This means that she _____ .

   a. has decided to do something

   b. has become furious

   c. has filled out the court papers

6. Janet dropped off the car Monday morning. This means that she _____ .

    a. forgot to deliver the car to the mechanic

    b. picked the car up Monday morning

    c. left the car with the mechanic Monday morning

7. Ted is going to confirm Janet's story in court. This means that Ted _____ .

    a. is going to verify her story

    b. is going to sue the mechanic

    c. is going to explain things to the mechanic

8. Janet is claiming $375. This means that she is _____ .

    a. losing $375

    b. complaining about $375

    c. asking for $375

9. Janet said, "I'm tired of getting stepped on by dishonest people. This means that _____ .

    a. it is hard for Janet to step on the clutch

    b. she doesn't want to be treated unfairly

    c. women shouldn't drive stick shifts

10. The mechanic had the nerve to tell Janet that she was wrong. This means that the mechanic _____ .

    a. was very nervous

    b. knew what he was talking about

    c. was very impolite

C.   Supposed to   Answer the questions in complete sentences. Use the present tense form of the verb **to be** + **supposed** + **infinitive**. Follow the example:

QUESTION: Will the car be ready by 4:00 P.M.?

ANSWER: I think so. It _is supposed to be_ ready by 4:00.

1. Will he show up in court on the court date?

2. Will he return her money?

3. Will the judge listen carefully to her case?

4. Will they bring a witness to court?

5. Will she fill out the court papers?

6. Will you claim less than two thousand dollars?

D.   Supposed to   Answer the questions in complete sentences. Use the past tense form of the verb **to be** + **supposed** + **infinitive**. Follow the example:

QUESTION: Did the mechanic fix the clutch?

ANSWER: No. He _was supposed to fix_ it, but he didn't.

1. Did you pay the court clerk a small fee?

2. Did her witness confirm her case?

3. Did their neighbor recommend a good mechanic?

4. Did she drop her car off on Monday?

5. Did they fill out the form?

6. Did they show up for their court date?

E.   Suing in small-claims court   Read sentence 1. What do you do next? Use numbers 2 through 8 to put the sentences in order.

_____ Fill out the forms and write the amount you're claiming.

_____ The defendant has a chance to respond and tell his or her story.

_____ You ask your witness to appear in court on the correct date.

_1_ You have to get the forms from the court clerk.

_____ You can tell your story in court.

_____ You have to pay a fee.

_____ The judge decides if the defendant is guilty or innocent.

_____ The marshal serves the papers.

F.   Could have + past participle   Practice these exchanges with a partner. Follow the example:

   A: I heard that you lost your court case.

   B: Yes, and I was so embarrassed that I
   ___could have died___ . (die)

   1. **A:** I heard that the mechanic wouldn't return your money.

      B: Yes, and I was so mad that I _____ him with his own screwdriver. (hit)

2. **A:** I heard that your witness didn't confirm your case.

   B: Yes, and I was so upset that I ＿＿＿＿＿＿ . (cry)

3. **A:** I heard that your neighbor recommended an awful mechanic.

   B: Yes, and I was so furious that I ＿＿＿＿＿＿ . (scream)

4. **A:** I heard that the judge didn't believe your story.

   B: Yes, and I was so unhappy that I ＿＿＿＿＿ him. (choke)

5. **A:** I heard that the judge ordered the mechanic to pay you.

   B: Yes, and I was so happy that I ＿＿＿＿＿ him. (kiss)

G. Conversation   How about you?

1. Have you ever gone to court? When? Why?

2. Have you ever had trouble getting your money back? Why?

3. Have you ever taken your car to an awful mechanic? What happened?

4. Have you ever recommended a mechanic, repair person, or handyman to a friend? What happened?

5. Tell about a time when someone made you very angry.

6. Get together with some other students and write a conversation about Janet's day in court. You'll need a judge, the mechanic, Janet Parker, and her husband, the witness.

CHAPTER 14

A Little Worse

Vocabulary

approach (v)   get near, come close

complain (v)   express unhappy feelings

drain (n)   hole in a sink or floor that leads to a pipe

paperwork (n)   desk work that involves forms and other papers

pour (v)   let flow (as coffee into a cup)

proof (n)   something that shows the truth

sour (adj)   spoiled or bad (as milk)

up-to-date (adj)   current, good for now

yawn (v)   open the mouth widely and take a deep breath

Idioms

She was dressed **in no time**.   very quickly, in a short time

Her alarm didn't **go off**.   ring (as an alarm)

It's all **in order**.   arranged, organized, correct

Can't you just **let me go**?   release from responsibility, forget it

143

A Little Worse

Nothing was going right for Janet that Monday morning. It all started when she woke up late because her alarm didn't go off. She didn't understand it. Her alarm was always set for 6:30 A.M. Every day.

Janet jumped out of bed and started the water running in the shower. She was trying to be quiet because Ted was still sleeping. He had the day off.

"That lucky guy," she thought, as she waited for the water to get hot. Janet yawned.

The water didn't get hot. She waited a little longer, but the water never got hot.

"I can't believe this," Janet complained. "I'm going to have to take a cold shower. Brrrrr!"

After her shower, Janet called the office and told her boss that she was going to be late for work. Janet was a responsible employee, and she didn't want anyone at work to worry about her. She said that she'd arrive as soon as possible.

It didn't take Janet very long to get ready. She was dressed, her hair was combed, and her makeup was applied in no time, but her stomach was upset. Janet decided that she'd better take a few minutes for breakfast.

"I'll have a quick one," she said to herself.

She took a box of Ted's natural grain cereal from the cabinet, and she poured herself a bowl of it.

"Ick!" Janet shouted. "This milk is spoiled." She poured the sour milk down the drain.

"I've got to get to work," she said to herself.

Janet is on the freeway. She's speeding. She's going seventy-five miles per hour. Janet hears a police car siren and sees flashing lights behind her. Janet pulls her car over to the side of the freeway. A highway patrolman approaches.

OFFICER: Good morning. May I see your driver's license?

JANET: Of course, Officer. Here it is.

OFFICER: Do you know how fast you were going?

JANET: Not exactly, Officer. I'm late for work, you see, Officer, and I've had a bad morning.

OFFICER: A bad morning, huh? Well, it's going to get a little worse, young lady. May I see your vehicle registration?

JANET: Yes. I have it here in the glove compartment. It's all in order. It was renewed last month.

OFFICER: And your proof of insurance?

JANET: Yes, of course. Here's my insurance card. It's all up to date. The insurance was paid months ago.

OFFICER: I'm glad to see that you have your seat belt on, young lady.

JANET: Oh, I always wear my seat belt. I wouldn't be caught dead without my seat belt on!

OFFICER: And did you know that your left taillight was out? It didn't light up when you stopped.

JANET: That can't be true, Officer. It was burned out a month ago, but it was fixed. My husband fixed it.

OFFICER: Okay. I'll let it go this time, but get it fixed again, young lady. Here's your driver's license, and here are your other papers. I'll need your signature on the ticket.

JANET: Oh, Officer! I can't believe this is happening to me. I've never had a ticket before in my life. Can't you just let me go? I won't speed again. I promise.

OFFICER: Sign here, please.

JANET: This is the worst day of my life! The alarm doesn't go off! No hot water! Sour milk! A speeding ticket! Late for work! And it's only 8:30!

OFFICER: That's too bad. Look, young lady. It's not my job to tell you this, but I will. You don't have to pay that ticket. You can get out of it by going to traffic school.

JANET: Traffic school? I don't understand.

OFFICER: You can call traffic court and have them send you all the information on traffic school. You pay the court a small fee for paperwork. Then you sign up for an eight-hour traffic class, which costs about thirty-five dollars. The traffic school instructor gives you a certificate at the end of the course. You deliver the certificate to traffic court, and everything is taken care of.

JANET: Everything is taken care of? What do you mean?

OFFICER: I mean that the ticket won't be put on your driving record, and your insurance won't be informed.

JANET: That's great! I can't thank you enough, Officer. You've been very helpful. I appreciate it.

OFFICER: That's okay. I hope your day gets better.

JANET: It just did, Officer.

Exercises

A.   Answer the questions in complete sentences.

1. Why did Janet wake up late?

2. Why was Ted still sleeping?

3. Why did Janet call her office?

4. Why did Janet pour the milk down the drain?

5. What did Janet hear and see behind her on the freeway?

6. What three things did the officer ask to see?

7. When was her vehicle registration renewed?

8. What was wrong with Janet's left taillight?

9. What did Janet have to sign?

10. What did the officer tell her about?

B.   True or false   Read each sentence. Write **T** on the line if the sentence is true. Write **F** on the line if it is false.

_____   1. A person yawns when he or she is tired.

_____   2. If a police officer lets you go, he gives you a ticket.

_____   3. A drain is a hole in a sink that lets the water go down.

_____   4. If your insurance is up to date, it is paid for.

———— 5. When an officer approaches you, he or she walks away.

———— 6. If your important papers are in order, they are organized.

———— 7. Your vehicle registration is proof that you own the car.

———— 8. If you complain, you're unhappy about something.

———— 9. You pour coffee into a cup.

———— 10. If you get ready in no time, you spend a lot of time getting dressed.

C.   **Passive voice**   Change each sentence to the passive voice. Use **is** or **are** and the past participle. Follow the example:

Officers give speeders tickets.

Speeders are given tickets.

1. She always sets her alarm.

2. She always combs her hair.

3. They throw away sour milk.

4. They renew their registration and insurance every year.

5. She keeps her papers in the glove compartment.

6. He always locks his car doors.

7. They make their coffee strong.

8. They pay their bills on time.

D.   Passive voice   Change each sentence to the passive voice. Use **was** or **were** and the past participle. Follow the example:

The officers gave the speeders tickets.

The speeders were given tickets.

1. She combed her hair.

2. She made her breakfast.

3. He renewed his vehicle registration last month.

4. They paid their house insurance and their car insurance two months ago.

5. Her husband fixed the headlight and the taillight.

6. I paid the court fee.

7. The officer gave her a speeding ticket.

8. The students studied all the rules.

E.   What do you think?   Read the sentences below and decide if what the person did was legal or not legal. Write **That's legal** or **That's illegal** on the line. If what the person did was illegal, explain why.

_____ 1. Janet made a right turn into the lane next to the center line.

_____ 2. There were no cars coming, so Ted crossed the street in the middle of the block.

_____ 3. Janet made a left turn from the left-turn lane when the arrow turned green.

_____ 4. You parked ten feet away from a fire hydrant.

_____ 5. Ted was going sixty-five miles per hour on a highway in the open country.

_____ 6. It was a little foggy, so Janet drove with her parking lights on.

_____ 7. You parked by a yellow curb because you were only going to be a minute.

_____ 8. Ted made a left turn into a parking lot. He crossed the double set of double lines in the center of the street in order to make his turn.

F.   Read sentence 1. What happened next? Use numbers 2 through 9 to put the sentences in order.

_____ The officer told Janet about traffic school.

_____ Janet poured the sour milk down the drain.

_____ Janet's day began to get better.

_____ The officer asked to see Janet's vehicle registration.

_____ Janet signed the ticket.

__*1*__ Janet woke up late because her alarm didn't go off.

_____ Janet asked the officer to let her go.

_____ Janet took a cold shower.

_____ The officer asked to see Janet's driver's license.

_____ Janet showed the officer her car insurance card.

G. **Conversation** How about you?

1. Have you ever gotten a ticket? Tell about it.

2. Have you ever been late for work or school? Explain.

3. Do you use an alarm clock? Why or why not?

4. How often do you speed on the freeway? Why?

5. Why do you think an officer asks to see a person's vehicle registration? And his or her car insurance?

6. Do you always wear a seat belt in the car? Why or why not?

7. Do you think that an eight-hour traffic class is a good idea? Why or why not?

8. If you were Janet, would you take this class? Why or why not?

CHAPTER 15

I'd Marry You

In this chapter you will recognize many of the vocabulary words and idioms that were introduced in chapters 1 through 14. The exercises will help you review grammar, vocabulary, and idioms.

As you complete the exercises, see if you can remember the situation in which a vocabulary word or idiom was first used. Think about the different events that occur in this novel.

Before you read this final chapter, think about the title "I'd Marry You." Look at the picture of Ted and Janet. What do you think the title refers to? Discuss with a partner what you think will happen in this chapter.

I'd Marry You

Ted and Janet ended up staying home on their third wedding anniversary. They were considering taking another weekend trip, but trips always cost an arm and a leg. They thought about going to a movie, but they couldn't decide what to see. Ted was looking forward to a delicious meal at a first-rate restaurant, but Janet didn't want to go out and eat like a pig. They were having trouble making up their minds, so they decided to stay home.

"We can do without a huge anniversary celebration, can't we?" Janet said. "Anyway, we should continue sticking to our budget. You don't mind, do you, honey?"

"I don't mind at all. I think it's great that you'd rather stay home and save money," Ted answered.

On the evening of their anniversary, Ted built a delightful fire and opened a bottle of champagne. Janet brought in a photo album. She wanted to sit in front of the fire and remember old times.

JANET: Oh, Ted. Look at this picture of you in front of our old apartment. Remember that place? It was the noisiest apartment complex in town.

TED: Yeah. We're living much more comfortably in this little rental house.

JANET: Look. Here's a picture of me on Fisherman's Wharf in San Francisco. I was beginning to put on a few pounds when we went there, wasn't I?

TED: We've both lost a lot of weight since that trip. We've been taking better care of ourselves for the last several months.

JANET: Look at yourself playing golf in this photo, Ted. Did you make that funny face on purpose? You look like a monkey.

154

TED: I was trying to make you laugh when you took that picture. Don't you remember how angry you were at me for always playing golf on the weekends?

JANET: I remember. I flew off the handle one weekend because you wouldn't pitch in with the housework. I dropped the laundry basket in the middle of the living room floor and left the house to get my own checking account.

TED: Uh-huh. You got that checking account for freedom and independence from me!

JANET: Well, why not? It's a free country. Hey! Look at this photo. You're wearing that unusual red and green tie. I gave that to you for Christmas. What happened to that tie, honey?

TED: The tie? The red and green tie that you gave to me? Well, um . . . Wow! Here's a great picture of you! This is the picture that I like the best. If I had only one photo to keep of you, I'd keep this one.

JANET: But what about the tie, Ted? You didn't throw it away, did you?

TED: Well, I wore it so much that it got worn-out. Really, honey.

JANET: Oh, Ted. You don't believe that, and I don't either. You could have told me that you didn't like it.

TED: Janet, this is our anniversary. Let's not argue about the tie. You know, if I had to get married all over again, I'd marry you.

JANET: Thank you, Ted, and happy anniversary, honey. How about some more champagne?

Exercises

A. Answer the questions in complete sentences.

1. Why didn't Ted and Janet take a weekend trip for their anniversary?

2. Why didn't they go to a first-rate restaurant?

3. What did Ted think of Janet's idea of staying home?

4. Why did Janet want to look at the photo album?

5. How long have Ted and Janet been taking better care of themselves?

6. Why did Janet fly off the handle one weekend?

7. What happened to the tie that Janet gave Ted for Christmas?

8. What didn't Ted want to do on their anniversary?

B. Grammar review Choose **a**, **b**, or **c** as the correct answer.

1. They thought about _____ to a movie.

   a. to go

   b. going

   c. go

2. Ted wanted to see a movie, but he couldn't decide _____ .

   a. what to see

   b. what he's seeing

   c. how to see

3. You don't mind if we stay home, _____ ?

   a. mind you

   b. don't you

   c. do you

4. That old apartment was _____ place in town.

   a. noisier than

   b. the noisiest

   c. the noisier

5. Ted and Janet were living much _____ in their rental house.

   a. most comfortable

   b. comfortably

   c. more comfortably

6. Janet _____ to put on a few pounds when they went to San Francisco.

   a. was beginning

   b. has begun

   c. begins

7. Since that trip, they _____ a lot of weight.

   a. lost

   b. were losing

   c. have lost

8. Ted was trying to make Janet laugh when she _____ that picture.

   a. was taken

   b. took

   c. has taken

9. He doesn't like the tie _____ .

    a. by Janet

    b. for which Janet gave him

    c. that Janet gave to him

10. If Ted had only one picture to keep of Janet, he _____ that one.

    a. would keep

    b. will keep

    c. has kept

C.   Grammar review   Circle the correct answer.

1. Ted and Janet wanted to live in (a/an/the) quiet house.

2. Are (a/an/the) utilities included?

3. Ted wanted to look at (a/an/the/X) inexpensive couch.

4. (A/An/The/X) sofa that the salesman showed them was cheap.

5. Their house is (the roomiest/roomier than) their old apartment.

6. They want to live on (the quietest/the most quiet) street in the city.

7. The salesperson showed them (the more expensive/the expensivest/the most expensive) sofa in the store.

8. Ted shops (carefully/most carefully/more carefully) than Janet.

9. He's a (terrible/terribly) dancer.

10. He dances (terrible/terribly).

11. The boss gave (Ted/to Ted) a nice raise.

12. I sent a card (her/to her) on her birthday.

13. They weren't saving any money, (were they/weren't they)?

14. She'll probably buy more shoes, (will she/won't she)?

15. I didn't tell you about the accident, (did I/didn't I)?

16. You have a new job, (do you/don't you)?

17. She was interested in (to find/finding) full-time work.

18. Most people don't enjoy (to get/getting) laid off.

19. Ted left the house (to/for) a golf date.

20. Dee gave Janet a signature card (to/for) fill out.

21. Ted (said/told) Janet that he would fix the faucet.

22. The plumber (said/told) it would be expensive.

23. (Did/Were) the Parkers thinking about moving?

24. (Did/Was) the faucet leak very much?

25. Ted hasn't gone golfing in a long time, and his friends (hasn't/haven't/has/have) either.

26. Janet doesn't want to do the laundry, and I (doesn't/don't/does/do) either.

27. Bleach isn't good for permanent press clothing, and neither (is/isn't) hot water.

28. He forgot to lock the back door, and so (did/didn't) she.

D. Review of idioms Find the word or phrase in column B that means the same as the idiom in column A. Write the letter of the correct answer on the line.

<table>
<tr><td align="center">**A**</td><td align="center">**B**</td></tr>
<tr><td>_____ 1. cost an arm and a leg</td><td>a. intentionally</td></tr>
<tr><td>_____ 2. look forward to</td><td>b. prefer</td></tr>
<tr><td>_____ 3. eat like a pig</td><td>c. contribute, help</td></tr>
<tr><td>_____ 4. make up your mind</td><td>d. old from use</td></tr>
<tr><td>_____ 5. do without</td><td>e. gain weight</td></tr>
<tr><td>_____ 6. would rather</td><td>f. decide</td></tr>
<tr><td>_____ 7. put on a few pounds</td><td>g. continue trying something</td></tr>
<tr><td>_____ 8. on purpose</td><td>h. overeat</td></tr>
<tr><td>_____ 9. fly off the handle</td><td>i. anticipate</td></tr>
<tr><td>_____ 10. pitch in</td><td>j. live without a certain thing</td></tr>
<tr><td>_____ 11. stick to something</td><td>k. be expensive</td></tr>
<tr><td>_____ 12. worn-out</td><td>l. get angry</td></tr>
</table>

E. Verb review Complete each sentence with the correct tense of the verb.

1. Their faucet _____ for a long time. (drip)

2. She _____ at a sewing shop when she _____ laid off.
   (work) (get)

3. In the future we _____ to stick to our budget. (have)

4. Her alarm _____ always _____ for 6:30 A.M. (set)

5. Their car insurance _____ last month. (pay)

6. Janet _____ since the boss's birthday dinner. (overeat)

7. Janet _____ the mechanic to small-claims court last month.
   (take)

8. Janet _____ with Ms. Lynch when the phone _____ .
   (speak) (ring)

9. Larry was full and _____ to finish everything on his plate.
   (not/be able)

10. If you put your red shirt in hot water, it _____ . (fade)

11. If I lived in a neighborhood with a lot of crime, I _____ part
    in a neighborhood watch. (take)

12. If Ted and Janet _____ dead bolts, they wouldn't feel
    nervous. (have)

13. If Ted _____ his sweater in the dryer, it will shrink. (dry)

14. I've been in the hardware store for fifteen minutes, but no
    one _____ me yet. (help)

15. They've been married for three years, but they _____ a
    baby yet. (not/have)

F. Word order   Make a sentence or a question by putting the words in the correct order.

1. you / carpets / steam clean / Will / the?

2. is / payment / penalty / There / a / miss / if / you / a.

3. cook / think / prepared / I / everything / wonderfully / the.

4. seats / you / vacant / tourist / in / have / the / Don't / any / class?

5. had / company / to / withholding / deduct / tax / government / for / The / federal / the.

6. cut / expenses / down / How / we / can / our / on?

7. on / bulletin / printouts / The / are / computer / the / boards.

8. balance / There / minimum / is / two-hundred-dollar / a.

9. Americans / years / doctors / For / said / many / have / too / meat / eat / red / that / much.

10. by / given / a / She / ticket / officer / speeding / was / an.

G.   Conversation   How about you?

1. Do you think Ted and Janet are happily married? Why or why not?

2. Why do you think Ted and Janet don't have any children yet?

3. When do you think they'll buy their own house? Why?

4. Who do you think has a stronger personality—Ted or Janet? Why?

5. Would you like to be married to Ted or Janet? Why or why not?